Draw Near

Draw Near

The Heart of Communion with God

SCOTT ANIOL

WIPF & STOCK · Eugene, Oregon

DRAW NEAR
The Heart of Communion with God

Wipf & Stock
An Imprint of Wipf and Stock Publishers
199 W. 8th Ave., Suite 3
Eugene, OR 97401

www.wipfandstock.com

PAPERBACK ISBN: 978-1-7252-6044-3
HARDCOVER ISBN: 978-1-7252-6043-6
EBOOK ISBN: 978-1-7252-6045-0

Manufactured in the U.S.A.   01/29/20

Contents

Introduction

KNOCK. KNOCK. KNOCK.

Who could that be at the door? you think. *I have so much to do—good things, necessary things. I'm too busy to answer.*

Knock. Knock. Knock.

A voice. *His* voice.

What does he want, now? You shrink back further into the house, hoping he won't know you're home. *This place is a mess, I can't let him come in.* You look around; your eyes linger on the locked door. *I certainly can't let him see in that room.*

Knock. Knock. Knock.

How long has it been since he was here last? In my home? At my table? You can't seem to remember. It's been a long time.

"My child," the voice says, firmly, but gently. "Open the door. I want to come in to you and eat with you, and you with me."

You walk gingerly toward the door. Your genuine love for him compels you to do so, even though you're ashamed.

You unlock the deadbolt and slide back the chain. You turn the handle and open the door, just a crack. He's standing at your door, a look of love and compassion on his face where you expect to find disappointment and judgment.

"It has been too long, my child. Let me come into your dining room." He has something in his hands.

"Look, I've brought the supper."

> Behold, I stand at the door and knock.
>
> If anyone hears my voice and opens the door,
>
> I will come in to him and eat with him,
>
> and he with me. (Rev 3:20)

Communion with God.

What comes into your mind when you hear that phrase—*communion with God?* Sitting cross-legged, eyes closed, arms outstretched, humming? Losing yourself in emotional ecstasy? Being ushered into another dimension? Centering rituals? Emptying your mind and hearing audible voices from God?

Maybe you've been drawn to ideas like this, always disappointed when you genuinely pursue God, and none of this happens. Or maybe popular perceptions like this have given you a distaste for the very notion of pursuing communion with God. *No,* you insist, *the Christian life consists simply in rational understanding of biblical theology and pursuit of holiness*; any talk of communion with God is mystical new age gibberish.

Through a series of meditations on several biblical passages, I want to show you that communion with God is not mystical or mysterious—rather, communion with God is rooted in the gospel of Jesus Christ, clearly communicated throughout the Scriptures, and absolutely vital for a fruitful Christian life that brings God ultimate glory.

There is perhaps a no more beautiful picture of the relationship that God desires to have with us as his children than how Christ expresses it in Revelation 3:20. The image of dining with another person around a table in their home, in the Ancient Near East, was about the best picture of intimate communion with someone you could use. You didn't just invite anyone into your home. You didn't just eat with anyone. You only invited to your dining table those with whom you had free and open fellowship.

This is what was pictured with the Table of Showbread in the tabernacle and temple in the Old Testament. That table symbolized communion with God in his presence. This is why at the end of all of the major corporate worship festivals in Israel, they had an extended time of feasting in God's presence. This is why in Psalm 23, the fact that God prepares a table before us *in the presence of our enemies* is so amazing and beautiful. It pictures the fact that he welcomes us into communion with him. This is also why the Pharisees were so upset when Jesus ate with publicans and sinners. They did not approve of Jesus so intimately communing with people so publicly scandalous. And one day, all of redemptive history will culminate in a great marriage banquet.

And yet, this leads to the question of why he's out on the front porch in the first place. Why isn't he already in your dining room eating with you?

1

The Call to Communion with God

THE MAN WAS A scoundrel, certainly not worthy of the invitation he had just received. He had stolen before—he had even stolen from the king's treasury. And now he was eyeing the fat purse on the richly-dressed nobleman headed his way on the main road, when he felt a tap on his shoulder.

Oh no, he though. *Caught at last.*

"Sir," a voice behind him said. He turned around.

"Sir, the king is giving a wedding feast for his son." This was clearly one of the king's servants. He continued, "He has prepared the dinner, his oxen and fat calves have been slaughtered, and everything is ready."

And what would someone like me have to do with that?

"The king would like you to come," the servant said. "Come to the wedding feast."

> And those servants went out into the roads
> and gathered all whom they found,
> both bad and good.
> So the wedding hall was filled with guests. (Matt 22:10)

LET US DRAW NEAR

Imagine—the sovereign, holy, all-powerful Ruler of the universe invites lowly, finite, severely flawed creatures into his presence.

This is exactly what he calls us to do. The end of Hebrews 10 contains such an invitation:

> Therefore, brothers, since we have confidence to enter the holy places by the blood of Jesus, by the new and living way that he opened for us through the curtain, that is, through his flesh, and since we have a great priest over the house of God, let us draw near with a true heart in full assurance of faith, with our hearts sprinkled clean from an evil conscience and our bodies washed with pure water. (Heb 10:19–22)

"Let us draw near."

This idea of drawing near is an important focus of the book of Hebrews, evident by its presence in the three major climaxes of the book. Here in chapter 10:22 we find the second of these climaxes. The first is found in 4:16, which says, "Let us then with confidence draw near to the throne of grace, that we may receive mercy and find grace to help in time of need." And the final climax of the book is 12:22, which says, "But you have come to Mount Zion and to the city of the living God, the heavenly Jerusalem, and to innumerable angels in festal gathering," and that phrase "you have come" is a translation of the same Greek term translated "draw near" in Hebrews 10:22.

Not only does this concept of drawing near appear in the book's main literary climaxes, but it also appears in several other places in the book as well. Hebrews 7:25, 10:1, and 11:6 all focus our attention on the call to draw near to God, the basis for drawing near, and the means for drawing near. The concept of drawing near is critical in this book.

So what is the importance of this command? What does "drawing near" mean?

This idea of coming or drawing near is a translation of a term that means more than just a casual coming toward something. Rather, it specifically refers to approaching God, and we can see this by how it is used in the book of Hebrews; we find commands to draw near to God, draw near to the throne of grace, and 10:19 implies that we are to draw near to the holy place of God's presence. So it is clear that this drawing near is coming to God, and throughout the book of Hebrews the author compares this idea of drawing near to the Hebrew worship practices—they are in chapter 10 as well, terms like "holy place," "the veil," "high priest," "sprinkling" and "cleansing"; drawing near to God is what the author defines as the essence of worship—communion with God.

Drawing near to God in worship permeates the storyline of Scripture. It is what Adam and Eve enjoyed as they walked with God in the cool of the day (Gen 3:8). Exodus 19:17 describes it when Moses "brought the people out of the camp to *meet God*" at the foot of Mount Sinai. He had told Pharaoh to let the people go so that they might worship their God in the wilderness, and this is exactly what they intended to do at Sinai. It is what Psalm 100 commands of the Hebrews in temple worship when it says, "Come into his presence with singing and into his courts with praise." It is what Isaiah experienced as he entered the heavenly throne room of God and saw him high and lifted up (Isa 6). To draw near to God is to enter his very presence, to bask in his glory, to fellowship with him. It is the plea of the psalmist when he says,

> One thing have I asked of the Lord,
> that will I seek after:
> that I may dwell in the house of the Lord
> all the days of my life,
> to gaze upon the beauty of the Lord
> and to inquire in his temple. (Ps 27:4)

KOINONIA

This idea of "drawing near" is a central picture of communion with God throughout Scripture, but the word most often translated "communion" or "fellowship" in the New Testament is the term *koinonia*. The core meaning of this term helps to further uncover the essential nature of communion with God.

At its root, *koinonia* simply means sharing something or having something in common with another person. For example, Luke uses the term to describe the "partnership" in fishing shared by Peter, Andrew, James, and John (Luke 5:10). Similarly, Paul uses the term to describe the sharing of material goods to meet the need of Christians in Macedonia (2 Cor 8:4).

This helps us begin to understand that communion is not something mystical or mysterious; rather, it is a relationship between individuals in which they share of themselves with each other.

TRI-UNITY

The Tri-unity of God presents the perfect example of, and is indeed the ultimate source of this concept of communion. God the Father, Son, and Holy Spirit, each individual and unique persons within the singular godhead, experience perfect fellowship one with another. The very truth of three-in-one and one-in-three reveals the amazing communion shared by the persons of God. Their communion is so complete that to divide their being would be to divide God himself; as persons they are distinct, but in essence they are One. Jesus himself tells us of the unique relationship that he has with his Father; it is a relationship so profound that in reality, no one knows the Father except the Son, and no one knows the Son except the Father (Matt 11:27).

This reality about God—something that is unique to the God of Scripture compared to the gods of other religions—provides the basis for all discussions of communion with God and with others. As we will explore in the chapters below, our commune with God is a reality in which all three persons of the godhead, each enjoying perfect communion one with another, play an active role.

CREATED TO COMMUNE

Indeed, to commune with God is to commune with his triunity; as John tells us, "Our fellowship is with the Father and with his Son

Jesus Christ" (1 John 1:3), and Paul explains that this fellowship is accomplished by the Holy Spirit: "For through [Christ] we both have access in one Spirit to the Father" (Eph 2:18).

That's right—God wants *you* to join in the communion he already shares within his own godhead.

Jesus himself described the relationship of one who believes in him to the triune God; notice this astounding language: "At that day you will know that I am in my Father, and you in me, and I in you" (John 14:20). "My Father will love him," Jesus promised for one who believes, "and we will come to him and make our home with him" (John 14:23). It's incredible that Jesus uses language of union here, parallel to the union he has with his Father. Later, John records a similarly striking statement Jesus made concerning the communion he desires for his people in relation to the shared communion among the persons of the trinity:

> That they all may be one, as you, Father, are in me, and I in you; that they also may be one in us, that the world may believe that you sent me. And the glory which you gave me I have given them, that they may be one just as we are one: I in them, and you in me; that they may be made perfect in one, and that the world may know that you have sent me, and have loved them as you have loved me. (John 17:21–23)

What an amazing description of the relationship God desires to have with us: "one in us"—one with the communion enjoyed by the persons of the trinity themselves.

In fact, God created Adam and Eve with the express purpose that they would join in the communion enjoyed by the persons of the trinity:

> Then God said, "Let us make man in our image, after our likeness." . . . So God created man in his own image, in the image of God he created him; male and female he created them. (Gen 1:26–27)

Possessing the image of God means that Adam and Eve—and us by extension—are *relational* beings; we have the capacity, and indeed the need to commune with others. God intended that Adam and

Eve would commune with each other—"it is not good that the man should be alone," and he intended that they together would commune with him—walking with him in the cool of the day.

INITIATED BY GOD

What all of this should immediately reveal is that communion with God is not something we initiate, create, work up, or generate in any way. We cannot call God down to us through some sort of ritual or ceremony, like Baal's prophets dancing around the altar crying out for their god to hear them.

No, God initiates the relationship of communion with him through a disclosure of himself. He first reveals himself through his creation: "His eternal power and divine nature have been clearly perceived, ever since the creation of the world, in the things that have been made" (Rom 1:20). However, as we will soon see, sin blinds us to what would otherwise be plain, causing us to "suppress the truth" (v. 18). It is only when God reveals himself to us that we can draw near to communion with him.

But this makes the invitation for us to draw to him even more amazing. Creating humankind with all the universe in itself displayed God's glory; he could have chosen to leave us to ourselves, imaging him through our lives. But he didn't. He chose to reveal himself to Adam and Eve, and he has chosen to reveal himself to us in his inspired Word.

And through that revealed Word, God calls us to do what we were created to do—commune with him.

DINING WITH CHRIST

As we have already seen from Revelation 3, communing with God is like eating with someone around your table in your dining room. In that kind of setting, you can let your guard down; there's no need for pretense. Dining with someone is an opportunity for you to listen to them, to get to know them, to enjoy their company. It is an opportunity to share your heart, to communicate something of yourself. There is a mutual give and take that happens around a table. You listen as the other person speaks, and then you respond in dialogue with that person. And as you do, your relationship with that person grows deeper as you get to know them better.

This should describe the nature of our relationship with God: dining with him. We listen intently as he speaks to us through his inspired Word. And our goal in listening to his words is not simply to gain more knowledge; our goal is to know him better, to learn his likes and his dislikes, to enjoy his company. And then we speak back to him; we tell him how much we love and adore him; we share something of ourselves and cast our burdens on him.

Communion with God, like dining with someone, is a dialogue: God speaks, we speak. And as we share this communion, our relationship with God grows deeper. This is why worship is profoundly relational; all true worship is communion with God. Jesus described this kind of dialogical nature of worship when he said to the Samaritan woman in John 4 that God desires those who will worship him in spirit (our response toward God) and truth (God's word to us).

And that is exactly what is pictured in Christ's invitation in Revelation 3:20. Here is the Son of God himself—verse 14 describes him as "the Amen," the affirmation and completion of all of God's promises toward us; he is the faithful and true witness and the source of all that is. This very Son of God stands at your door knocking, desiring to come into your formal dining room to eat with you in intimate communion.

Think about how amazing this really is. Verse 14 uses some pretty lofty language to describe Jesus:

> The words of the Amen, the faithful and true witness, the beginning of God's creation.

This is language not meant to emphasize the humanity of Christ, although he is without doubt 100 percent human. This language is meant to highlight his divinity. He is "the Amen" of God. Paul said in 1 Corinthians 1:20, "For no matter how many promises God has made, they are 'Yes'—Amen in Christ." He is the "faithful and true witness"—"He who has seen me has seen the Father" (John 14:9),

Jesus said. He is the "radiance of the glory of God and the exact imprint of his nature, and he upholds the universe by the word of his power" (Heb 1:3). He is the "beginning"—the source and ruler—of all creation.

He is transcendent, he is all powerful, he is the beginning and the end, the Alpha and Omega, the source, sustainer, and end of all things, the King of Kings and Lord of Lords. Revelation portrays him as one with brilliant white hair, flaming eyes, a long white robe with a golden sash, bronze feet, and a voice like the roar of many waters. When John saw Christ in all his glory, he fell flat on his face in terror (Rev 1:12–17).

And yet this same majestic, almighty Sovereign is standing at your door. And he wants to come into your house, into your dining room, to sit at your table and fellowship with you.

2

The Basis for Communion with God

THE KING RAGED WITH fury.

How dare they say I have no right to be here? he steamed. *I have done right in the sight of God. He has blessed me.* He thought of all the rich spoils of battle adorning his chambers. *I have grown strong. My fame has spread far. I deserve to be here.*

"My lord, you must leave!"

What is his problem? How dare he say I must leave? The king picked up the censor to burn incense on the altar. *I am trying to honor the Lord with this.*

The priest persisted. "It is not for you, Uzziah, to burn incense to the Lord, but for the priests, the sons of Aaron, who are consecrated to burn incense."

The king turned. A crowd of strong priests stood behind Azariah in the doorway.

The priest moved a step closer. "Go out of the sanctuary," he pleaded, "for you have done wrong, and it will bring you no honor from the Lord God."

How dare he challenge the Lord's blessed servant? He lowered the censor toward the altar.

He trembled, the censor dropping from his hand. *What is that?* White scales appeared all over his outstretched hand. His left leg collapsed beneath him. A sharp pain spread across his forehead.

King Uzziah was a leper until the day of his death.
He dwelt in an isolated house, because he was a leper;
for he was cut off from the house of the LORD. (2 Chron 26:21)

BARRIERS

Let us draw near.

The Son of God himself invites you to draw near to the presence of God and enter into the eternal communion enjoyed by the three persons of the triune godhead.

But any reader of the invitation in Hebrews to draw near would have immediately recognized its inherent problem—this God to whom we are supposed to draw near is holy; he cannot tolerate sin. Yet we are sinful.

The fall of mankind into sin destroyed the possibility of drawing near to God. After Adam and Even sinned they no longer enjoyed the privilege of walking with God in the garden; instead they hid from him in fear and desperately tried to cover their guilt with leaves. And ever since that time, any attempt to draw near to God results in a profound recognition of guilt and unworthiness.

The Israelites experienced this when they drew near to Mount Sinai; when they witnessed the majesty and greatness and white-hot holiness of God, they trembled in fear and begged Moses to go in their behalf. This is the reason that although God inhabited the holy place in the tabernacle and later the temple, no person could enter his presence except the high priest once a year on the Day of Atonement. This is what Isaiah experienced when he saw the Lord high and lifted up in all of his glory and holiness and cried out with, "Woe is me! For I am lost; for I am a man of unclean lips, and I dwell in the midst of a people of unclean lips; for my eyes have seen the King, the Lord of hosts!" (Isa 6:5).

Second Corinthians 4:3 says that every person is born in the condition of perishing, and thus the beauty of a relationship with

God is veiled to us: "And even if our gospel is veiled, it is veiled to those who are perishing." Even worse, Paul says that "the god of this world has blinded the minds of the unbelievers, to keep them from seeing the light of the gospel of the glory of Christ, who is the image of God" (v. 4). All people are perishing and blind; all people are depraved. The Bible says that no one seeks after God (Rom 3:11); the natural mind cannot understand the things of God (1 Cor 2:14). And because of this, perishing, blind people do not even recognize the wonder and beauty of communion with God.

The problem with the command in Hebrews 10 is that we have neither the right nor even the desire to draw near to God; we do not have access to him because of our sin. The only way God enabled people to partially draw near to him is through temporary sacrifices, and even then there are barriers keeping us from the very presences of God himself; there is a veil hiding the holy place, only the high priest can enter there and only once a year, and we know what happens if you even touch the symbol of God's presence, the ark—Remember Uzzah? Even Psalm 100 calls people to come only into the outer courts of the temple, not into the actual presence of God. The people had no direct access.

The point is that we cannot obey this command. God commands us to draw near, but this entering into the presence of God to worship him is not possible.

Or is it?

THROUGH CHRIST

Hebrews 10 explains the solution to the problem through two "since" clauses. The first is found in verse 19: "Since we have confidence to enter the holy places . . . draw near." Now the term translated "confidence" in most English translations has the idea of free and open "access" to someone or something. "Since we have access to enter the holy places . . . draw near." So this verse is specifically addressing our problem. God commands us to draw near to him, but because of our sin we do not have access to him. Yet this verse tells us that such access *is* possible; it *is* possible to have access to the holy place of God's presence.

Here is the first term in our text that is meant to conjure up images of Old Testament worship. The holy place was that most sacred of places in the tabernacle and temple, and several boundaries prevented access to God in this place. The first was the wall that enclosed the outer court of the temple, then was the wall of the temple itself, and finally the veil that hid the holy place where the Ark of God dwelt. In each successive stage, fewer and fewer people had access. No Jew would ever even consider entering the holy place; they knew what happened when Uzziah did that.

In fact, if you go to Jerusalem today, you'll find out that there's a certain area of the temple ground where it is forbidden for Jews to ever walk, because it may be the area where the Holy of Holies once stood, and no Jew would ever put his foot on the Holy of Holies. So that's why there are big signs outside the gates of the temple area that say, "Orthodox Jews have been forbidden by the rabbi to enter in this place lest they step on the Holy of Holies." Orthodox Jews have a fear still today of ever going into the presence of God.

Jesus our Substitute

But Hebrews 10:19 tells us that we have access, not just to the outer court, not just into the entrance of the temple, but beyond the veil into the very presence of God. How can this be? Keep reading: "by the blood of Jesus, by the new and living way that he opened for us through the curtain, that is, through his flesh."

Access to God is possible through a sacrifice, and this is no ordinary sacrifice; this is the vicarious, substitutionary atonement of the Son of God. At the beginning of Hebrews 10, the author revealed the insufficiency of animal sacrifices to purify those who come to God in worship: "For since the law has but a shadow of the good things to come instead of the true form of these realities, it can never, by the same sacrifices that are continually offered every year, make perfect those who *draw near*."

But this sacrifice *can* perfect those who draw near. This Jesus is fully man, and thus he can stand as our substitute, and he is fully God, and thus he can pay an eternal punishment to an eternal, holy God that no normal man could. And because of the perfection and eternality of this sacrifice, it need not be offered day after day after day to atone for sin; it is offered *one time* and the complete wrath of God is fully appeased.

This is what God pictured when he slew the animal in the garden and covered Adam and Eve's guilt. This is what was pictured when Moses offered a sacrifice at the foot of Mount Sinai so that the elders of the people could approach God. This is what was pictured each year in Israel on the Day of Atonement when an animal was sacrificed and the high priest entered the holy place to sprinkle blood on the mercy seat. This is what was pictured when the seraph took a burning coal from the altar and placed it on Isaiah's lips, saying, "your guilt is taken away, and your sin atoned for."

And this is pictured perhaps no more beautifully than with what happened at the moment of Christ's death. The gospel accounts of the crucifixion tell us that Jesus cried out with a loud voice and gave up his spirit, and at that exact moment, the veil of the temple was torn in two, as if that veil was the body of the Son of God himself prohibiting entrance into the presence of a holy God, and that access that had been lost by the fall of man is now restored! There is now a new and living way to draw near to God, and that way is his Son.

This phrase, "new and living way," paints a beautiful picture as well. The word translated "new" here is not the typical word that would have been used to describe a new coat or a new chariot. It is a word that literally means "freshly slaughtered." He was freshly slaughtered and yet he is living! He rose from the dead, having defeated sin and death. And now we have access to enter the holy place by the blood of Jesus by a freshly slaughtered, yet living way—Jesus Christ.

Therefore, draw near.

Jesus our High Priest

But there is another "since" clause that explains to us how we have access to God, and that is found in verse 21: "and since we have a great priest over the house of God . . . draw near." In the Old Testament economy, the only person on earth allowed to actually enter the presence of God, and that only once a year, was the high priest. But this verse tells us that not only is Jesus the perfect sacrifice that gains us access to God, but he is also the high priest who offers the sacrifice; and now because of our relationship to this Great High Priest, we can draw near to God. Hebrews 7:25 emphasizes the fact that Christ's high priestly ministry of intercession makes such an approach possible: "Consequently, he is able to save to the uttermost those who *draw near* to God through him, since he always lives to make intercession for them."

So God commands us to draw near to him in worship, but this is only possible through the shed blood of Christ on our behalf and through Christ's high priestly ministry. Jesus Christ is the only basis for drawing near to God in worship.

Jesus Came to Restore Communion

This was exactly the purpose for which Jesus came to earth. John 1:14 tells us that "the Word became flesh and dwelt"—literally "tabernacled"—"among us." He was given the name "Immanuel: God with us"—since sinful people could not dwell in the presence of a Holy God, God came to dwell among sinful people for the purpose of restoring the communion lost by the fall.

Notice what Jesus says in his prayer to the Father in John 17:

> Father, the hour has come; glorify your Son that the Son may glorify you, since you have given him authority over all flesh, to give eternal life to all whom you have given him. And this is eternal life, that they know you the only true God, and Jesus Christ whom you have sent. I glorified you on earth, having accomplished the work that you gave me to do. And now, Father, glorify me in your

own presence with the glory that I had with you before the world existed. (John 17:1–5)

Jesus says that he has accomplished the mission the Father gave him to glorify the Father, and what is this work that he had been given to do by the Father? He summarizes it first in verse 2: "to give eternal life to all whom the Father had given to him." Christ's mission was to redeem a people through his perfect life, his sacrifice of atonement, and his victorious resurrection.

But it wasn't simply redemption for its own sake, as verse 3 explains: "And this is eternal life, that they *know you*, the only true God, and Jesus Christ whom you have sent." The purpose of the redemption accomplished by Jesus was that this redeemed people would *know* the only true God, and Jesus Christ his Son. The purpose of Jesus's mission was that these redeemed people would have restored communion with God that had been broken by sin, that they would worship and glorify him against whom they rebelled. This, according to Jesus, is the definition of eternal life—communion with God.

And so Jesus's mission was essentially to create worshipers out of sinners through his shed blood on the cross and his defeat of sin and death made manifest by his resurrection. This brought glory to himself and ultimate glory to God the Father.

But Jesus continues in verse 6 to further explain the work he was given to do. First, he made God known; he "manifested God's name." He displayed the glory and the magnificence of the Father in ways that no one else could because he *is* God; if you have seen the Son, you have seen the Father. And so through his life, his actions, his character, and ultimately his death and resurrection, Christ made God known.

But he did not make God known only through his actions; notice what he says at the end of verse 6: "they"—that is, those whom the Father gave to the Son; those to whom he granted eternal life; those to whom he made God known—"they have kept *your word*. Now they know that everything that you have given me is from you. For I have given them *the words* that you gave me."

Jesus made God known through the proclamation of God's Word. And that proclamation led to belief: "and they have received [that Word] and have come to know in truth that I came from you; and they have believed that you sent me." That Word Jesus proclaimed—the Word that had been given to him by the Father—was the means through which his people believed in him and trusted in him as the source of forgiveness, eternal life, and ultimately communion with God. It was not enough for him to accomplish atonement or make God known through his actions; people are saved only through faith, and faith comes by hearing, and hearing by the Word of God. The only way his people would come to know him was through proclamation—proclamation of the glorious good news of redemption made possible through the shed blood of Christ.

So how does Jesus describe his own mission? The mission of Jesus was to glorify God by accomplishing atonement and making God known to his people through his life and through the proclamation of God's Word, which is the basis for restoring communion with his people.

LET THERE BE LIGHT!

So what, then, is the solution for those who are in the condition of perishing, those whose sin prevents them from drawing near to the presence of a holy God, those who are blinded to the beauty of such communion? Paul explains the solution in 2 Corinthians 4:6:

> For God, who said, "Let light shine out of darkness," has
> shone in our hearts to give the light of the knowledge of
> the glory of God in the face of Jesus Christ.

God is the only one powerful enough to break the blinding power of Satan and depravity and reveal the beautiful light of the gospel to unbelievers! Paul uses the perfect illustration in this text to rid us of any doubt. If God had the power to create physical light out of darkness, then surely he has the power to illumine hearts so that they apprehend the beauty of communion with God.

Think about the amazing power and might that God displayed in the first chapter of Genesis. From eternity past there was nothingness. There was no light, there was no space, there was no mass, there was not even time. Only God existed.

And then amidst the silence and the darkness and the nothingness there came the voice of Almighty God saying, "Let there be light," and there was light! God did not require tools or materials or anything outside of himself. All it took was the authoritative, irresistible command from his lips, and light appeared.

And this very same God, this God who created light with mere words, is the same God who said "I will call out a people for my name's sake," and who said "I will have mercy on whom I will have mercy, and I will have compassion on whom I will have compassion" (Exod 33:19). And what God says, he will do. If he had power to shine light out of dark nothingness, then he has the power to shine light in dark hearts.

And when he does this, when God illuminates the heart, then the beauty of the gospel of the glory of Christ is revealed!

It's as if men are groping around in a pitch black cave desperately searching for the treasure that they know to be there but cannot find. And then suddenly a spotlight is shown directly in front of them to reveal a magnificent diamond that was there the whole time. All men are born in blackness. They are blinded as to the beauty of the gospel of Christ. They are empty, they are searching. In their heart of hearts they know that there must be something that will satisfy their longings, something that will fill the void in their souls. But they are unwilling and unable to accept that it is God himself who will satisfy that longing, God himself who will fill that void. All they must do is submit to God as King and they will find that treasure. But they hate God and they reject their knowledge of him. They are unwilling to submit to the gospel because they do not recognize the beauty of the glory of Jesus Christ.

But then just as God created light at the beginning of time, with just his voice he says, "Let there be light," and light shines on a dark heart. And when that happens, that perishing person looks up and sees the truths of the gospel literally in a new light. No more does he see mere facts about a man who once lived and died. No longer does he see God as a terrible taskmaster. No longer does he see the demands of the gospel as unreasonable. That light that has been shined upon his heart reveals the magnificent beauty of the gospel of the glory of Jesus Christ.

When such an illumined person apprehends the beauty of the gospel, he is drawn irresistibly to its splendor. No one turns away once he has seen the beauty of the gospel. Such a miracle of illuminating the heart inevitably results in salvation, because when a person really sees the beauty and value of the knowledge of the glory of God, he cannot help but give himself entirely over to that God.

And ultimately, this beauty and glory and value is revealed in the very face of Jesus Christ. He is the beauty. He is the glory. He is the value. And when someone sees Christ for who he really is, he will fall down on his face before Christ and say, "What would you have me to do?"

The apostle Paul experienced such a miracle in a very literal sense. Before Paul submitted to Christ, he persecuted Christians and imprisoned them and killed them. He knew about the gospel, he knew about Jesus Christ. In fact, Paul was a very religious man. But he hated Christ, and he hated the gospel. Maybe this describes you. You know the truths of the gospel, but you are unwilling to submit yourself to them.

But then one day as he was traveling to a city in order to take Christians as prisoners, a light from heaven flashed around him. Paul fell to the ground, and at that moment he recognized the beauty of the gospel of Jesus Christ and submitted himself to whatever God had for him.

Have you seen the beauty of the glory of the gospel of Christ? Have you seen its value? Have you recognized its worth?

You may know the truths of the gospel. You may even believe the historical facts of Jesus Christ. But Satan believes these as well. Yet he certainly does not submit to Christ, and you do not submit to Christ. Why? Because you have not recognized the beauty of Christ. You do not value Christ above all else. You do not worship Christ.

What is holding you back from submitting to Christ? Do you not see that communion with God is worth far more than wealth or prestige or freedom or even family or friends? And it is certainly of more value than the temporary pleasures of selfish sinful indulgence. Turn away from those things. Turn to Christ who is the source of all-satisfying joy and beauty and pleasure!

This is the source of communion with God—Someone hears the truths of the gospel, God supernaturally shines light into his heart so that he recognizes the beauty and value of the gospel of the glory of Christ. And when that happens to a person, he will give up everything for Christ; he will value Christ above all else. That is true Christianity. Is that you? Has God shone a light into your heart so that you recognize the beauty of fellowship with Christ?

3

The Means to Communion with God

I CANNOT BE HERE. I should not be here.

He knew he was unworthy. He could hardly lift his head.

The sound was almost deafening. "Holy, holy, holy is the Lord of hosts!" It was a sound unlike he had ever heard before, yet also strangely familiar. Terrifying, yet comforting all at the same time. "The whole earth is full of his glory!"

He raised his hand to shield his eyes from the brilliant light. They were still there, these fearsome beings he had only imagined as a child. He peered past them to the figure sitting on the throne, high and lifted up. One glance, and he was flat on his face again.

"Woe is me!" he murmured as he rose tentatively to his knees, his head still low, his arms raised in desperation. "For I am lost; for I am a man of unclean lips, and I dwell in the midst of a people of unclean lips; for my eyes have seen the King, the Lord of hosts."

He felt a movement of air and saw out of the corner of his eye a figure move swiftly to his left. He glanced up. One of the beings was doing something at the altar. It turned, and the man lowered his face once again in fear.

He felt a presence hovering above him. A strong hand took his arm and pulled him to his knees. The being raised his hand in which he held a burning coal from the altar. He placed it on the man's lips.

A sharp, burning sting struck the man, but quickly it turned to a comforting warmth that spread down his face into his body. He felt somehow stronger, somehow refreshed.

Somehow forgiven.

"Behold," the being said, "this has touched your lips; your guilt is taken away, and your sin atoned for."

> In the year that King Uzziah died
> I saw the Lord sitting upon a throne,
> high and lifted up;
> and the train of his robe filled the temple. (Isa 6:1)

BY FAITH

Communion with God is possible only through the atoning sacrifice of Jesus Christ and his high priestly ministry on our behalf. And without the life-giving power of the Holy Spirit, we wouldn't even recognize the beauty and value of such communion.

Yet all of this work on God's part to draw us into communion with him does not mean we have no responsibility for the relationship. Communion is two-way; yes, God's work on our behalf is foundational, but we have a role as well.

We've seen how Hebrews 10 clearly articulates the God-initiated basis for communion with him, but the passage also tells us the means of drawing near. The text commands us in verse 22 to "draw near with a true heart in full assurance of faith." The basis for drawing near to God is the sacrifice of Christ, but the means of drawing near is sincerity and faith in Christ.

"True" in the text literally means "real" or "sincere." God does not want worshipers who draw near out of duty or habit. He desires those who will draw near with sincerity out of a deep longing for communion with him.

But not only are we to draw near with a sincere heart, we are also to draw near in full assurance of faith. Hebrews 11:6 emphasizes the need for faith in coming to God in worship: "And without faith it is impossible to please him, for whoever would draw near to

God must believe that he exists and that he rewards those who seek him." This is the essence of faith: belief in what we cannot see.

So faith is absolutely necessary in order to draw near to God, and this is essential to our understanding of the nature of communion with God. Faith, according to the author of Hebrews, is "the assurance of things hoped for, the conviction of things not seen" (11:1). You see, the God to whom we are drawing near in worship is one whom we cannot see. We cannot see him, we cannot touch him, we cannot feel him; we do not experience God with any of our physical senses, and so the only means to approach him in worship is with faith—with full assurance that he exists and that he rewards those who seek him; with full assurance he will keep his promise that if we draw near to him, he will draw near to us.

Am I Really Worshiping?

However, this drawing near in faith is difficult for us for at least two reasons. First, we are physical beings and so we want physical proof that we are truly communing with God. We naturally want to be able to point to something, whether it is a location or a ceremony or a tradition or a ritual or a feeling, and say, "That's worship." And so when we attempt to obey this command to draw near to God in worship and nothing physical happens, we begin to doubt. Have I really drawn near? Am I in the presence of God? Am I really worshiping?

And then we end up needing other things to give us confidence that we're really worshiping, whether it be a certain kind of stimulating music or an atmosphere that creates a certain aura, or a particular place; and if we don't have those things, then we don't "feel" like we're worshiping. But the author here commands us to draw near to God with a true heart in full assurance of *faith* in things we do not experience with the physical senses.

If we cannot draw near to God in worship simply with nothing more than faith in him, then perhaps we are not worshiping at all. As Christians, we worship by faith and not by sight. We worship by faith and not by feeling.

Am I Really Worthy?

But the other reason we may have difficulty drawing near is because of guilt. Any one of us who is genuinely honest acknowledges that even as children of God, when we consider the prospect of drawing near to the presence of God, we know that we are not worthy. Even just a few moments ago you may have snapped at your children or ridiculed your spouse or broken the speed limit or had a demeaning thought about someone else; how dare you assume that you can just waltz in to the presence of God? Who do you think you are?

Hebrews 10:22 tells you who you are: If you are a follower of Christ, you are one who has had your heart sprinkled clean from an evil conscience and your body washed with pure water. The term translated "evil" in the text literally has the sense of condemning or guilty. These expressions are flavored with Old Testament purification ideas; your guilty conscience has been cleansed; your filthy sinful flesh has been washed; this assures you that no matter who you are, no matter what you have done, even five minutes ago, if you are in Christ, God accepts you; you have every right to draw near to God because of Christ. We can sing with Charles Wesley, "Arise, my soul, arise! Shake off your guilty fears. A bleeding sacrifice in your behalf appears!"

This is why each week, when believers come together to draw near to God corporately, they should acknowledge their sinfulness toward God but then find assurance of pardon in the gospel: "In Christ your sins are forgiven!" We have been reconciled to God; his pardoning voice we hear; with confidence we now draw nigh and Father, Abba Father cry.

IN THE SPIRIT

Before Christ, the prospect of drawing near to God was a fearful thing; after Christ, there is nothing more joyous. The author of Hebrews displays this contrast beautifully at the end of chapter 12. There the author contrasts the Hebrews drawing near to God at Mount Sinai with Christians drawing near to God at Mount Zion, the heavenly Jerusalem.

> For you have not come [drawn near] to what may be touched [remember, we worship, not my sight or touch or feeling], a blazing fire and darkness and gloom and a tempest and the sound of a trumpet and a voice whose words made the hearers beg that no further messages be spoken to them. For they could not endure the order that was given, "If even a beast touches the mountain, it shall be stoned." Indeed, so terrifying was the sight that Moses said, "I tremble with fear." (Heb 12:18–21)

This is what drawing near to God looks like if you are unworthy of drawing near. The Hebrews resisted it; they begged that God stop speaking—it was terrifying. There was severe judgment connected to this kind of worship—if you did something wrong, you would be killed. Even an animal who touched Mount Sinai would be stoned. Moses himself trembled with fear when God revealed himself in this way.

But the author says that as Christians we have not come to that mountain; rather, we have access to heaven itself:

> But you have come [drawn near] to Mount Zion and to the city of the living God, the heavenly Jerusalem [to that which you cannot see or feel or touch], and to innumerable angels in festal gathering, and to the assembly of the firstborn who are enrolled in heaven, and to God, the judge of all, and to the spirits of the righteous made perfect, and to Jesus, the mediator of a new covenant, and to the sprinkled blood that speaks a better word than the blood of Abel. (Heb 12:22–24)

Because of the sprinkled blood of Christ, we have access to the holy place of the heavenly temple; we have access to God himself. Notice that the response is entirely different for those who have a right to draw near to God. This worship is a festal gathering; it is a joyful assembly in the presence of God and his angels and other believers and Jesus Christ himself.

You are a thoroughly sinful person—if you're honest with yourself, you know this—but if you are a Christian, God does not see you that way. No matter what you do, no matter how awful you are, no matter how much you mess up and sin and do terrible things, if you have been clothed in the righteousness of Christ, that is all God sees. "No condemnation now I dread; Jesus and all in him is mine!" And so you can draw near to communion with God through Christ by faith with full boldness.

We are now enabled to ascend to God and worship him in heaven through Jesus Christ; not physically, but spiritually. And this is where the third person of the triune God—the Holy Spirit—does another work. Scripture teaches that along with regenerating perishing, blind hearts, the Holy Spirit of God unites those who draw near in faith to Christ at the moment of their conversion, and thus it is in the Spirit that we are enabled, through Christ, to draw near to the heavenly temple. Ephesians 2:18 explains this most succinctly:

> For through [Christ] we both have access in one Spirit
> to the Father.

Paul explained earlier in the chapter that when we placed our faith in Christ, God "raised us up with him and seated us with him in the heavenly places in Christ Jesus" (Eph 2:6). Thus, we draw near to communion with God through Christ in the Spirit by faith. Paul expressed it this way in 2 Corinthians 3:14:

> The grace of the Lord Jesus Christ and the love of God
> and the communion of the Holy Spirit be with you all.

This is exactly what Jesus had promised his disciples when he told them he would send the Holy Spirit. The third person of the godhead would be "God with us" in Christ's absence, not only because of his own divine presence, but also because in the Spirit we would forever be united to Christ himself:

> And I will ask the Father, and he will give you another
> Helper, to be with you forever, even the Spirit of truth....
> You know him, for he dwells with you and will be in you.
> I will not leave you as orphans; I will come to you.
> (John 14:16–18)

ABIDE

As Christians who have placed our faith in the atoning sacrifice of Christ, we are seated in the heavenly places through Jesus Christ; we have access to the very center of God's presence in the Spirit where we can commune with him. Nothing can separate us from this communion (Rom 8:39).

Yet, since in this life we still experience sin, we must continue to cultivate our relationship with him. We are *positionally* in union with Christ, and nothing can separate us from him—not even our sin; nevertheless, we must *remain* in communion with Christ throughout our lives. John 15 is one of the most vivid pictures of how we ensure our continual communion with God through Christ:

> I am the true vine, and my Father is the vinedresser. Every branch in me that does not bear fruit he takes away, and every branch that does bear fruit he prunes, that it may bear more fruit. Already you are clean because of the word that I have spoken to you. Abide in me, and I in you. As the branch cannot bear fruit by itself, unless it abides in the vine, neither can you, unless you abide in me. I am the vine; you are the branches. Whoever abides in me and I in him, he it is that bears much fruit, for apart from me you can do nothing. (John 15:1–5)

In this passage, Jesus paints a beautiful picture of our communion with him by using an extended metaphor. The image of a vineyard would have been very familiar to the disciples. Vineyards were prevalent in the land; we don't know for sure, but perhaps Jesus was speaking this as they walked from the Upper Room to the Garden of Gethsemane, and they stopped at a vine just as he began this discourse.

In a vineyard, the vine was the source of all nourishment and, ultimately, all fruitfulness, for it was the vine that had roots in the soil. No branch would be nourished or produce fruit that was not vitally connected to the vine. And so the vine became a very common metaphor for the source of blessing.

So Jesus makes clear, he is the true vine; he is the true source of all spiritual nourishment and blessing. It is only when we continually remain vitally connected to Christ as the true vine that we will be fruitful. You see, there are important priorities in our lives that Christ himself emphasized during his earthly ministry, but the key to fruitfulness in these matters is that there is something even more important, more central, that must be our first priority above even these other good emphases.

Christ explains it with three simple words in verse 4: "Abide in me."

What must a Christian do to be vitally connected to Jesus? Abide in him.

What must a Christian do to cultivate communion with Christ? Abide in him.

So what does it mean to abide in Christ, and how do we do it? "Abide" here simply means to remain. It is really that simple. Remain in Christ.

Now notice, if you are a true branch, then you are already vitally connected to the true vine. If you are truly a Christian, then you are already in Christ. When you believed in Christ, the Holy Spirit of God united you to him (1 Cor 12:12–13)—this is what is pictured in believer's baptism, and "there is now no condemnation for those who are in Christ Jesus" (Rom 8:1). That is a reality that cannot change for true Christians.

Yet although all Christians are already vitally connected to Jesus Christ, we nevertheless must maintain that vital connection. That is what Jesus is commanding here: *Abide in me. You are already in me, but it is your responsibility to remain in me.* Not that you can ever be separated from Christ, but the degree to which you abide in Christ is what is in view here. In other words, abiding in Christ is a condition of all true believers. The issue is degree.

But notice also from verse 4 that not only must we maintain our vital connection to Jesus Christ, but we are also equally required and responsible for Jesus to abide in us: "Abide in me, and I will abide in you." The command is connected to the result. To the degree that we maintain our communion with Jesus Christ, Jesus Christ will be vitally connected to us. As Christians, we will always be in Christ, and he will always be in us, but the more that we nurture and cultivate that relationship, the more we will experience the results of our union with him.

And what are those results? Very simply, fruit. Jesus makes this clear in the rest of verses 4 and 5. Fruitfulness is impossible without abiding in Christ. Unless we abide in Christ, we will bear no fruit, and the degree to which we are abiding in Christ determines the degree of our fruitfulness.

DIALOGUE

Now, this is all well and good, but we have yet to fully grasp how we do this. How do we abide in Christ—how do we commune with him? This is where Christ's transition from the extended metaphor to the explanation in John 15:7 is helpful. This verse is Christ's simple explanation of what it means to abide in him:

> If you abide in me, and my words abide in you, ask whatever you wish, and it will be done for you.

He first clarifies what it means for him to abide in us. Remember, in verse 4, he just commanded us to abide in him, and he in us. Now in verse 7 we find almost the same statement, only this time he uses different words to describe him abiding in us. What does it mean to abide in Christ? Verse seven tell us in other words: "If you abide in me, *and my words abide in you.*"

What does it mean for Christ to abide in us? Don't look for some mystical meaning. Christ abiding in us doesn't mean that we somehow empty our minds and wait for a kind of euphoria or ecstatic experience. Christ abiding in us simply means that his words abide in us.

You want to know how to cultivate this mutual abiding? Do you want to know how to commune with God? The beginning, very simply, is to hear from him. Allow his words to abide in you. And how do you do that? By reading, studying, memorizing, and meditating upon the Bible—God's words to us.

This is why Jesus said earlier that we are responsible for the degree to which he abides in us. He is not going to force himself upon us; he is not going to visit us in a dream or give us a vision or physically appear to us or somehow mystically fill us. The degree to which Christ abides in us is dependent upon how much of his words we fill into our minds and hearts.

But notice the second part of his explanation in verse 7: "Ask whatever you wish, and it will be done for you." After we fill ourselves with Christ's words—after we listen to him speak—the natural response is to speak back to him. This mutual abiding is dialogical in nature. God speaks—we speak.

This makes perfect sense if we take this idea of abiding and extend it to another metaphor. I mentioned earlier that to abide means to remain or to dwell. To abide with Christ and he abide with us is to *dwell* with him. Mutual abiding has the idea of living together in a common dwelling. Another word for that might be a *commune*. What are we doing when we dwell together with others? We commune with them. And what does that look like? What does it really mean to commune with someone? Again, this is not mystical. To commune with someone simply means they speak to us, and we speak back to them. They share themselves with us, and we with them. We dialogue, and thus nurture a mutual relationship and fellowship. And we have already seen this in the metaphor Christ uses in Revelation 3—dining with Christ, which communicates the same idea of having a conversation with someone over a meal.

To abide with Christ and he with us is really no more complicated than that. God speaks—we speak. Read your Bible—allow his words to dwell in you—and pray—allow your words to dwell in him.

This is abiding: it is fellowship; it is communion; *it is worship*.

LIVING SACRIFICE

God has called us to enjoy rich communion with him, and he has provided the only means possible for us to draw near to him. This is grace. This is mercy. And based on that grace and mercy, we should draw near to God in worship.

And when we do—when we offer ourselves to God in worship, the results are literally transformative. This is exactly what Paul explains in Romans 12:

> I appeal to you therefore, brothers, by the mercies of God, to present your bodies as a living sacrifice, holy and acceptable to God, which is your spiritual worship. 2 Do not be conformed to this world, but be transformed by the renewal of your mind, that by testing you may discern what is the will of God, what is good and acceptable and perfect. (Rom 12:1–2)

The primary command in this passage is found in verse 1: "present your bodies as a living sacrifice." Paul intends for this command to paint a picture in our minds, a picture of a lamb being offering on an altar to the Lord. We as Christians are to offer ourselves to the Lord just like Old Testament Jews offered lambs as sacrifices—this is what it means to worship God with our lives.

And notice the basis for this sacrifice. Paul says that he appeals to us, "therefore," directing our attention back to the first eleven chapters of Romans, which explore the great doctrines of salvation. In other words, he once again centers the motivation for worship in the grace of the gospel.

Not only is this sacrifice of ourselves based in God's grace, it is also a living sacrifice. Typically, something that was sacrificedno longer remained alive! But in the case of a Christian, we offer ourselves as a *living* sacrifice. This implies that this sacrificing of ourselves is a continual, progressive, day-by-day sacrificing. Every moment of our lives as Christians should be one of sacrificing ourselves to God. Every choice we make, every thing we do, every thought we have should be offered to God as a sacrifice of worship.

In this sense, the entirety of our lives should be a pursuit of communion with God. Worship is not just limited to Sunday mornings. Congregational worship is a special time set apart for God, but we can and should worship the Lord when we are driving, when we are shopping, when we are reading, and when we are listening to music or enjoying recreation. All of it is the Lord's.

The text says also that our sacrifice must be holy. To be holy means to be set apart. As Christians, we must set ourselves apart for God. As we offer ourselves as living sacrifices to him, we are demonstrating to him that every part of our lives is set apart for his glory.

This is the kind of sacrifice that God accepts. But it is not acceptable to God because we are so holy; we're not. Even as Christians our actions are stained by sin. Again, this sacrifice is acceptable to God because of Christ's sacrifice; it is Christ's sacrifice by which we are clothed in his righteousness and therefore acceptable to God. In other words, it is not our sacrifice that makes us acceptable. It is the fact that we are acceptable to God because of Christ's sacrifice that should motivate us to sacrifice ourselves to God.

Do Not be Conformed

Offering ourselves as sacrifices to God comes in two steps. First, Paul admonishes us: "Do not be conformed to this world." Conformity to the world means loving the things of this life—good things and bad—that crowd out our communion with God. Notice what John warns is the heart of worldliness:

> Do not love the world or the things in the world. If anyone loves the world, the love of the Father is not in him. (1 John 2:15)

As we will see later, love of the world prevents communion with God.

Be Transformed

Rather, we are to be transformed. What is to be transformed? Our values, our desires. How are we to be transformed? By the renewing of our mind. And how does that happen? Second Corinthians 3:14–18 reminds us that being renewed in our mind requires two things:

> But their minds were hardened. For to this day, when they read the old covenant, that same veil remains un-lifted, because only through Christ is it taken away. Yes, to this day whenever Moses is read a veil lies over their hearts. But when one turns to the Lord, the veil is re-moved. Now the Lord is the Spirit, and where the Spirit of the Lord is, there is freedom. And we all, with unveiled face, beholding the glory of the Lord, are being trans-formed into the same image from one degree of glory to another. For this comes from the Lord who is the Spirit.

First, we must be regenerated by the Holy Spirit—he must shine the light of the gospel of the glory of Christ in our hearts. And second, we must immerse ourselves in the Scriptures, beholding the glory of the Lord. We must fill our lives with things that express biblical values and that display the glory of God to us. It is only then that we will grow in our fellowship with Christ.

And so, God invites us to draw near to him, and this defines the essence of our communion with him. Christian worship is drawing near to God through Jesus Christ in the Spirit by faith. And when Christians do draw near to God, his promise is full com-munion with him. Draw near to God, and he will draw near to you, James says. He has invited you to come, and he has provided you the access through his Son by the power of his Spirit.

So come. Enjoy a rich communion with God through Jesus Christ.

4

The Heart of Communion with God

THEY TRIED TO MAKE her leave. She knew she shouldn't be here, but she loved him deeply, a love that came from a heart of desperate need.

He didn't turn her away, though. He watched as she wiped away the tears that had dripped onto his feat as he reclined at table. Then she pulled out the small jar from the folds of her gown.

She heard a gasp. "That must have cost a fortune," she heard someone exclaim. Indeed it had; it cost her everything.

She tapped the top of the flask on the stone floor. It cracked, filling the room with its strong fragrance. She carefully poured the smooth liquid on the master's feet, and once gain wiped them gently with her hair.

"Why was the ointment wasted like that?" someone else scolder her. "For this ointment could have been sold for more than three hundred denarii and given to the poor."

Another man, a religious leader, scoffed. "If this man were a prophet, he would have known who and what sort of woman this is who is touching him, for she is a sinner."

It was only then the master lifted his face from what she was doing and turned to the others reclining around the table. "Leave her alone. Why do you trouble her?" He looked back to the woman, love in his eyes. "She has done a beautiful thing to me."

> Therefore I tell you, her sins,
> which are many, are forgiven—
> for she loved much.
> But he who is forgiven little, loves little. (Luke 7:47)

ABIDE IN MY LOVE

Jesus taught in John 15 that abiding in Christ—communing with him—is as simple as allowing his words to abide in us and our words to abide in him. God speaks to us through his Word, and we speak back to him in prayer.

But this is not just listening and talking out of duty, like a husband who murmurs "Yes, dear" behind a newspaper as his wife tells about her day. In John 15:9 Jesus compares the essence of fellowship he desires with the kind of fellowship he shares with the Father:

> As the Father has loved me, so have I loved you. Abide in my love. If you keep my commandments, you will abide in my love, just as I have kept my Father's commandments and abide in his love. These things I have spoken to you, that my joy may be in you, and that your joy may be full.

To abide in Christ is to abide in his love. This is a relationship of love. It is hearing from Christ and speaking back to him out of a heart of love and devotion to him, a fellowship that results in *full* joy.

In other words, Christ describes the nature of our relationship with him, not in terms of a legal contract or duties performed, but rather in terms of the heart's affection for him.

FAITH PROOF

In his first epistle, the Apostle Peter expands upon this idea by identifying what it is that really proves we are communing with God. The Christians to whom he wrote were enduring intense persecution for their faith. In 1 Peter 1:6, he says that though these believers will most certainly rejoice in the reality of their new life in Christ, they will have to face various trials. And the reasons for these trials as revealed in the following verses give us an answer to the question of what will prove if our faith is indeed true:

> In this you rejoice, though now for a little while, if necessary, you have been grieved by various trials, so that the tested genuineness of your faith—more precious than gold that perishes though it is tested by fire—may be found to result in praise and glory and honor at the revelation of Jesus Christ.

Peter leaves no question as to the primary reason for trials in the lives of believers—so that their faith may be proven genuine. One who has only intellectual belief without real saving faith will buckle and fail under pressure. But the person who has true faith will come out from the trial proven genuine.

So what is it, exactly, that causes someone who is truly in fellowship with Christ to endure suffering, when false faith would crumble? In verse 6, Peter observes what truly constitutes a strong relationship with Christ: "In this you rejoice." Then after he notes their successful pass through the trials, listen how he describes them in verse 8:

> Though you have not seen him, you love him. Though you do not now see him, you believe in him and rejoice with joy that is inexpressible and filled with glory.

This is profoundly important for our understanding of what constitutes the heart of communion with God; it is not intellectual beliefs, though belief in the gospel is necessary to draw near to him, and it is not good works, although fruitfulness will result from true fellowship with God. Peter's discussion about true communion with God through faith being proven through trials is bookended in verses 6 and 8 with a description of the characteristic of true faith that allows it to stand firm under pressure—*affection for God*. Peter says, "You rejoice in your salvation!" "You love Christ even though you do not see him!" "You are filled with an inexpressible and glorious joy!"

This is the nature of saving faith—giving up self and houses and family and possessions and prestige and success for something so much infinitely better—affection for Christ.

THE GREATEST COMMANDMENT

The centrality of affection for God is exactly what Jesus taught in Matthew 22 when he was discoursing with the religious leaders of the Jews. They were vigorously testing him, trying to get him to slip so that they could slander his growing reputation. They ask the Lord, "Teacher, which is the great commandment in the Law?" By this question, they hoped to trap Jesus into emphasizing one or another of the commandments of the Law, thus allowing them to criticize his lack of emphasis in another. But Jesus responded without hesitation, and the answer he gave was not what they had expected:

> And he said to him, "You shall love the Lord your God with all your heart and with all your soul and with all your mind. This is the great and first commandment." (Matt 22:37–38)

The greatest commandment, according to Jesus, that for which we were created, is actually very simple: love the Lord your God. This is the heart of communion with God.

Jesus quoted the central statement of faith in the Old Testament, found in Deuteronomy 6:5. In Hebrew the word for "love" referred to an inclination of the whole person, the determined care for the welfare of something or someone. It might well include strong emotion, but its distinguishing characteristics were the dedication and commitment of choice. It is the love that recognizes and chooses to follow that which is righteous, noble, and true, regardless of what one's feelings in a matter might be. It is the Hebrew equivalent of the Greek *agapao* in the New Testament. This word has the same sense of intentional, purposeful, and committed love that is an act of the will. This love for God is different than the emotion and tender affection that we might feel for a child or a friend. This love for God is different than physical, sensual love. This love is a purposeful inclination of the mind and will.

Christ's primary intent here is to emphasize that this love for God should involve every part of who we are. To the ancient Hebrews, "heart" referred to the core of one's personal being. It is the inner self, the whole person. The book of Proverbs says that out of the heart "flow the springs of life" (Prov 4:23). This is not just intellectual assent; it is an intense, willful love from our whole being. The term "soul" refers to the inward, spiritual essence of a person. It is the same word that Jesus used when he cried out in the Garden of Gethsemane the night he was arrested: "My soul is deeply grieved, to the point of death" (Matt 26:38). Our love for God should be at the center of our very being. "Mind" implies loving the Lord with intellectual energy and strength. This means actively engaging our minds and understanding in the things of the Lord, and we come to know God through listening to him in his Word.

So you see, at the heart of our communion with God is that we love him with our entire being. God doesn't desire empty words or empty rituals. He wants our personal affection. He wants affection that is directed to him and not thoughtless emotion that takes more pleasure in itself than in him.

GOD-GLORIFYING HEART RESPONSE

Yet in a sentimentalist, emotionally-charged day and age, it is critical that we consider carefully the exact nature of our heart's affections toward God, because we can so easily define that nature of our communion with God in terms of feelings that actually glorify self more than they do God.

The Bible describes many different kinds of appropriate affections toward God that constitute the heart of our communion with him; we've already seen at least two of them—joy and love, but there are others, including contrition, peace, lament, gentleness, and so forth.

Yet there is one affection characteristic of God-glorifying worship that is often more emphasized in Scripture than the others, possibly because it reveals the nature of affections that truly glorify God rather than personal, self-gratifying feelings. Second

Corinthians 4:15 highlights this most important expression of communion with God, helping us to understand the character of affections that truly bring ultimate glory to him:

> For it is all for your sake, so that as grace extends to more and more people it may increase thanksgiving, to the glory of God.

Here Paul explains that he was willing to endure any trial or hardship in his proclamation of the gospel "for your sake"—for the sake of the Corinthians to whom he ministered. This appears to be a very human-centered, human-focused reason. But then at the end of the verse he says that he did it "to the glory of God." So which is it? Did he minister for people, or did he minister for God? What Paul says in between these two statements explains the relationship between "for your sake" and "to the glory of God" and reveals the affection central to communion with God.

First, Paul explains that ministering the gospel for their sake helped to extend God's grace to more and more people. Paul ministered the gospel to the Corinthians because it is through the clear preaching of the good news of Jesus Christ that God spreads his grace. As we have already noted earlier in 2 Corinthians 4, it is God's gracious work of regeneration that shines the light of the glory of Jesus Christ in dark hearts and draws them to faith in him. And this is exactly why Paul says in verse 15 that he ministered the gospel among the Corinthians. He did it for their sake so that God's grace would extend to more and more people.

Now what is this grace that Paul is talking about? Sometimes grace is defined as undeserved favor. It is favor that God shows to people who do not deserve it. It is a gift given to someone who has not done anything to earn or merit it.

But grace is really even more significant than that. Grace is not simply *un*deserved; grace is actually *ill*-deserved. In other words, grace is a gift given not just to one who doesn't deserve it; it is a gift given to someone who deserves the opposite. Grace is giving the silver to Jean Val Jean after it has been discovered that he stole the silver. It's not just that he didn't deserve the silver; he actually deserved to be imprisoned for theft, and yet grace gave him what he ill-deserved. Grace is Aslan giving his very life for Edmund's free-dom even though it was Edmund's treachery against Aslan that had enslaved him to the White Witch.

And grace is the Son of God dying on behalf of a people who hate and reject him. This grace is what spread to more and more people as Paul ministered the gospel. In this passage, it is the free gift of salvation that God gives to people who are ill-deserving. As we have already seen, verse 3 tells us that all people are in the condition of perishing; all people are blinded by sin and Satan; they reject God, and they sin continually against him. They deserve judgment and condemnation.

And yet God, in his grace, shone in our hearts to give the light of the knowledge of the glory of God in the face of Jesus Christ. Like the Corinthians, our blinded eyes were opened, our dark hearts were enlightened, and we recognized the beauty of the glory of Jesus Christ and found forgiveness from our sins through faith in him, restoring rich communion with God.

And so, as Paul preached the unadjusted gospel for the sake of the Corinthians, this ill-deserved favor spread to more and more people. Yet this still seems very human-centered. What is it about doing ministry for the sake of people, what is it about God showing grace to people that have rejected him, that brings him ultimate glory?

The answer is in the verse: "so that as grace extends to more and more people *it may increase thanksgiving*, to the glory of God." You see, the link that turns grace into glory is *gratitude*. Or, to put it another way, the affection of gratitude toward God for his grace in our lives is what brings ultimate glory to him. Paul knew that ministering the gospel of God's grace to as many people as possible would be used by God to extend grace to more and more people; and as that grace extended to more and more people, Paul knew that it would increase gratitude, which is what gives God the su-preme glory.

Now what is it about the nature of gratitude that brings so much glory to God? Why is it that gratitude connects the grace that he has shown ill-deserving sinners with his own glory? It is in answering this question that the centrality of gratitude in communion with God will become apparent.

Gratitude is a response to grace. God acts in grace, and we respond in gratitude. In particular, gratitude is a response of our affections toward God. It is very similar in many ways to responding with love toward God or joy or praise. These are spiritual affections with which we respond in communion with him when he has shown favor toward us.

But notice that Paul didn't say that what brought God most glory was increase of love toward him as grace extends to more and more people or increase of joy or praise. God's grace in our lives certainly does produce those affections, and God is certainly glorified when love and joy and praise toward him increase. But I believe that there is a particular reason Paul focuses on gratitude here instead of other affections.

Nothing More Than Feelings

You see all true spiritual affections have an object, and their object is always God. This is why true spiritual affections are different from what we often mean when we talk about our feelings. Feelings are different than affections. Feelings often have no object; mere feelings wallow in themselves. When we experience mere feelings apart from spiritual affections, our focus is not on any object; our focus is purely on ourselves and the feelings themselves. We love the feeling of love; we delight in the feeling of joy.

So sometimes we just feel happy, and someone might ask, "Why are you happy?" And we reply, "O, I don't know; No reason; I just feel happy." But that's different from spiritual affections at the heart of our communion with God. Affections always have an object; they always have a reason.

The problem is that sometimes we use the same word to describe both an affection and a feeling. For example, "love" could describe the affection we express towards a spouse, a child, or the Lord because we value them. This affection has an object and it is directed toward that object. This love is more about an inclination toward the object and a commitment we have toward that object that it is about a particular feeling. The feelings may come and go, but true love endures all things.

But the word "love" can also describe a warm feeling we have. And even though that feeling may be directed toward a particular object, we tend to enjoy the feeling for itself rather than the object of the feeling. Love in this respect is something people fall in and out of. When the feeling passes away, we say that we are no longer "in love." What we describe as joy, or even praise, is very similar. We could mean an affection we have toward an object, or we could mean a mere feeling we enjoy for itself. Often we mean both.

The thing about the affection of gratitude is that there really is no feeling we associate with it. I mean, think about it: what is the "feeling" of gratitude? And, by definition, gratitude always has an object. The object is always the focus of gratitude. So you might say, "I just feel happy, but I really don't have any particular reason." But you would never say that about gratitude. If you "feel" grateful, there is always a reason. You always feel grateful toward someone because of something they did for you or something they gave you or simply because of who they are.

With this understanding we are beginning to see why Paul would choose the affection of gratitude as that which connects God's grace to his glory instead of something like love or joy or praise. But before we develop that further, I want to look at two more ways gratitude is different than other affections.

Unlike most other feelings, gratitude isn't something you can artificially work up through external means. If you feel sad, you can work up happiness through something external like upbeat music or funny entertainment. In that case there really is no object of the happiness; you just feel happy because the music or the entertainment made you feel happy. We do this regularly in our lives.

But how do you work up gratitude? You can't really. It has to have a reason; it has to have an object. That distinguishes gratitude from just about every other kind of affection.

Finally, remember that we are talking about affection that we give to God in response to his gracious gift to us. Now it is true that getting a gift from someone often produces in us other kinds of emotions like joy, but isn't it often the case that when that happens, we direct the joy toward the gift instead of the giver? When someone gives us something, we often are filled with happiness, but sometimes we're mostly happy about the gift rather than the one who has given us the gift—someone gives you a new car, and you delight in the car; you love the car. This is even often true with the gift of salvation, unfortunately. God gives us the gracious gift of free forgiveness from sin, and we are happy about that, but often we are mostly happy that we don't have to go to hell, or we're more happy that we get to spend eternity in heaven than we are actually happy in God.

Gratitude never works this way. We could never direct gratitude toward a gift. You don't say "thank you" to the car you've been given; by definition, by essence, the affection of gratitude is directed toward the giver.

So the reason I believe Paul chose to focus on gratitude as the link between grace and glory is that while love or joy or praise could certainly be directed toward God as a result of his grace toward us, many times what we call love or joy or praise are actually mere feelings that are more about us or the gift than the one who showed grace toward us.

This is why true and genuine gratitude always glorifies God. If God shows grace toward us, and we are truly grateful, that gratitude inherently has God as its object, and it inherently acknowledges that we are undeserving of the gift. This glorifies God. Attempting to love God or take joy in God—which we should do of course— often results in narcissistic indulgence wherein we love the feeling of love or joy rather than God. But gratitude never works that way. By definition and essence, gratitude is a humble acknowledgement of our unworthiness to receive the gift and a profound exaltation of the giver. God said in Psalm 50:23, "The one who offers thanksgiving as his sacrifice glorifies me."

We often think of praise or joy or love as the ultimate expressions of worship toward God. We expect that true worship will be characterized by intense emotion and heightened praise and excited joy. But really, the affection most associated in Scripture with worship is actually something perhaps less flashy, less viscerally intense, and less directly connected to particular feelings; the affection most associated in the Bible with worship is gratitude.

Listen to how God characterizes Christian worship at the end of Hebrews 12:

> Therefore let us be grateful for receiving a kingdom that cannot be shaken, and thus let us offer to God acceptable worship, with reverence and awe, for our God is a consuming fire.

The heart of communion with God is a response of all that we are to the grace that he has shown to us; it is a recognition of our unworthiness that leads to unspeakable love and inexpressible joy as we hear him speak and express our hearts to him.

5

The Strengthening of Communion with God

IT WAS A STRONG vine, surging with health and life.

The vine dresser moved along the length of the vine, carefully fingering each branch. He had come to know these branches through the years. He knew their needs and tended to them with the love of a father.

He stopped. He reached in and touched a brittle branch, concern growing on his brow. *No good,* he decided. *This one is gone; no fruit. It's not abiding in the vine.* He cut it away and tossed it into the pile ready for burning.

He continued down the vine, stopping again after a few moments. *Why, this branch is struggling,* he observed. He carefully pushed aside the growing fruit showing signs of distress. *Ah,* he said with a smile. *There is still life here—just a few sucker shoots I need to prune.* Tenderly, he snipped away the little sprouts that were draining away the rich nutrients from the vine that the branch so desperately needed to produce fruit.

Just as he turned back toward the vine, something caught the vine dresser's eye. A broad grin spread across his face as he moved forward toward the large cluster of bold, rich fruit. He plucked off one grape and flipped it into his mouth, the sweet juices filling his senses.

> I am the vine; you are the branches.
> Whoever abides in me and I in him,
> he it is that bears much fruit,
> for apart from me you can do nothing. (John 15:5)

EVERYTHING WE NEED

Like any earthly relationship, cultivating communion with God is hard work; it's work with rich rewards, but work nonetheless. And the fact that *this* relationship is different than other earthly relationships makes it more difficult in that we cannot see or hear him with our physical senses, which is why we must draw near continually by faith.

But on the other hand, communion with God is easier than earthly relationships in that one party of the relationship is holy; there is only one person who can hinder the fellowship. Even more than that, God has given us everything we need to draw near to him; as Peter says,

> His divine power has granted to us all things that pertain
> to life and godliness. (2 Pet 1:3)

This is an amazing truth! This divine power is the same power that created the universe; it is the same power that raised Jesus from the dead. And this same power is the guarantee of the gift; the source assures the effectiveness of the gift. This guarantee is also demonstrated by the use of the word "granted." This word is in the perfect tense, which stresses permanence. This word is stronger than just "give"—it has certainty and assuredness tied to it. Because Christ's divine power is the source of this gift, we can be assured of its effectiveness to do what God intends it to do.

So what is this gift that Christ's divine power grants to us with all certainty? "All things that pertain to life and godliness." The word "godliness" is actually a compound of two words: "well" and "worship"; it is often translated "piety" or "devotion." Taken together, "life and godliness" refers to a pious life devoted to God above all else, the essence of communion with God. This kind of life does not come naturally to the human heart, which is why these "precious and very great promises" (v. 4) must be granted by God.

You see, although a life devoted to God is difficult for sinners, this verse clearly tells us that we have been given everything we need for godliness. We have no excuse. We can never say, "I can't help sinning because I don't have what it takes to be godly; the attractiveness of other loves is just too strong." No. If you are a true believer—if you have been given new life by Christ's divine power, then you also have been given everything you need for godliness.

LISTEN TO GOD SPEAK

Now, how does Christ accomplish this? How does he grant spiritual life and godliness to people? The verse continues, "through the knowledge of him who called us to his own glory and excellence." You see, we don't receive this gift of unreserved devotion to God unconsciously. It's not like we're just zapped without our knowledge or involvement. No, this gift comes through intentional, spiritual involvement on our parts—through our *knowledge* of God.

Think about it for a second: this is really no different than how we cultivate and strengthen other relationships—we make effort to truly *know* them by listening to them speak and observing their actions. It's the same with our communion with God. If we want to strengthen and nurture our communion with him, then we must listen to him speak and observe his actions—we must come to truly *know* him. And the good news is that unlike some people who are difficult to get to know, God has given us everything we need to know him in his all-sufficient Word.

I cannot stress this enough: there is no communion with God without faithful, fervent, devotional reading of his Word. Not reading just to gain information, settle theological disputes, or get advice for life, but reading in order to truly *know* God.

Partakers of the Divine Nature

And when we increasingly grow in our knowledge of God, Peter tells us in verse 4 that we "become partakers of the divine nature." Now this is a shocking statement, and I think Peter meant it to be. He wants us to realize the wonder of what happens through our personal knowledge of God. We are becoming partakers of the divine nature.

So what does it mean to be "partakers of the divine nature?" The word "partakers" here is very instructive for our discussion; it is a translation of the term *koinonia*, the word most often translated "communion" throughout the New Testament. In other words, being a "partaker of the divine nature" is exactly what Jesus had promised in John 17:

> The glory that you have given me I have given to them,
> that they may be one even as we are one, I in them and
> you in me, that they may become perfectly one."

To partake in the divine nature is to share such a fellowship with God that we come to resemble him in thought, word, and deed.

Have you ever noticed that two people who spend a lot of time together, especially seasoned married couples, often begin to resemble each other? Their mannerisms, vocal inflections, and facial expressions start to all be alike. The same is true when we faithfully devote ourselves to knowing God as he communicates himself in his Word—we will become like him. Here again it is the Holy Spirit that makes such a partaking of the divine nature possible. As we pursue communion with God by beholding his glory communicated to us in his Word, we are "transformed into the same image from one degree of glory to another. For this comes from the Lord who is the Spirit" (2 Cor 3:18).

The next phrase in 2 Peter 1 further explains what results when we commune with God: being partakers of the divine nature means that we escape the corruption in the world caused by evil desires. Corruption is the opposite of the divine nature. To be partakers of the divine nature means that we can escape sinful corruption; all of the sinful allurements of this world pale in comparison to our love and devotion to God.

So the truth about the nature of our spiritual lives is this: Christ's divine power has granted to us all we need for a life of devoted communion with him through our personal knowledge of him in his Word. It is through this knowledge that we commune with the divine nature, which enables us to escape sinful corruption.

Pursue Communion with God

But as Peter makes clear, we must fervently pursue this kind of communion with God. Peter says in verse 5, "Make every effort." He sets the tone right away by insisting that communion with God is not passive. No, nurturing a life devoted to communion takes effort, diligence, and hard work. We must, as Peter admonishes, add to our faith virtue, knowledge, self-control, steadfastness, godliness, brotherly affection, and love (vv. 5–7). It is only when we actively pursue qualities that characterize the divine nature that our knowledge of him will bear fruit.

SPEAK TO GOD

And then, just like any relationship, along with listening, observing, and striving to be like God, we must speak to him. Remember, communion is a dialogue; it is sitting across the dining room table from Christ, enjoying an intimate conversation; it is letting Christ's words abide in us and ours in him. Communion with God is reading the Bible and prayer.

Paul gives us a powerful example of such prayer in Ephesians 3:14–19:

> For this reason I bow my knees before the Father, from whom every family in heaven and on earth is named, that according to the riches of his glory he may grant you to be strengthened with power through his Spirit in your inner being, so that Christ may dwell in your hearts through faith—that you, being rooted and grounded in love, may

> have strength to comprehend with all the saints what is
> the breadth and length and height and depth, and to know
> the love of Christ that surpasses knowledge, that you may
> be filled with all the fullness of God. (Eph 3:14–19)

Here Paul is kneeling before the Father, specifically requesting from God what is necessary to cultivate regular communion with him.

Permanent Residence

Paul has several related requests that build upon each other, the first centering on his desire that Christ would dwell in our hearts. Now what is it that Paul is praying for here? Is he talking about the indwelling that comes with salvation? Well he can't be, because he is praying for believers. So Christ already dwells within us. Romans 8:9 says that if anyone does not have the Spirit of Christ, he does not belong to Christ, and 2 Corinthians 13:5 reiterates that Christ dwells within believers.

So he is not talking about initial, salvific indwelling. The word translated "dwell" here is a compound word that literally means to "settle down." I think that gives us an excellent picture of what Paul is requesting. When you move into a new house, it's never until several months after you move that you really feel settled in. You own the house, you control the house, you live in the house. But there are boxes everywhere, and you don't know where everything is, and everything does not yet have its place. But once you do get everything (or mostly everything) where you want it, you are able to really settle down in your home.

This is what Paul is praying for. If you are a believer, Christ dwells within you; he controls your life. But has he yet really put everything in order? Has everything in your life been put in its proper place? Are the rooms of your life free of clutter that might compete for a position of prominence? Is Christ really able to settle down in your life? I think all of us would have to say "no" to one degree or another. Every one of us has that secret closet or hidden room that Christ technically owns and controls, but hasn't really settled down in yet. What Paul is praying for is that Christ will be able to really settle down in us.

Now notice what part of us Paul specifically mentions as the place where Christ needs to settle down—in our hearts. This refers to our spiritual side, our loves, to our values, to what we delight in, the center of our communion with God. In other words, this is exactly our concern in this chapter, that our hearts would be strengthened such that we can enjoy communion with God. And notice what is required before Christ will be able to really settle down in our hearts: Paul says that this will happen through faith, just as we saw in Hebrews 10. The same unreserved trust that we place in Christ at our salvation is the same trust that we must place in him every day. For a Christian, faith is a way of life, not just a one-time decision for salvation.

But even if we do have faith, we can't just decide one day to set things in order so that Christ can settle down in our hearts. This must be a work of the Spirit. As Paul prays, God's Spirit must strengthen our inner man so that Christ can settle down in us. What is our inner man? The inner man is our regenerated self. It is really another way of saying our hearts—our spiritual beings. It is only when the Spirit strengthens our inner man that Christ is able to settle down in our hearts.

Now this is not some kind of mystical experience. The Holy Spirit is not going to zap us with some kind of power through which we will be strengthened. This is the day in, day out working of the Holy Spirit in our lives to sanctify us. And the primary means he uses to do so is his Word. In other words, just as it is the life-giving power of the Spirit that opens our blind eyes to the beauty of communion with Christ, and it is the Spirit who unites us with Christ, seating us in the heavenly places with him, so it is the Spirit of God who continually strengthens our hearts so that we can enjoy regular communion with God. Remember, communion with God happens through Christ *in the Spirit* by faith.

But notice the final phrase that qualifies this first request at the end of verse 17—"being rooted and grounded in love." When Christ is really settling down in our hearts, we will be rooted and grounded in love for him. We have already considered how the heart is the seat of our values, our delights, and this phrase bears that out. Christ's settling down in our hearts grounds us in love for him. And this really gets to the heart of Paul's first request. This is the kind of love for Christ that welcomes him to settle down in our hearts. This is an exclusive kind of love. This is the kind of love that lets Christ set in order all of our other lesser loves. This is the kind of love that values him above all else; it pushes out all other idols.

So Paul's first request is that God would strengthen our inner man with might through his Spirit that Christ may really settle down in our hearts, being rooted and grounded in our love for him.

Knowing Christ's Love

But notice Paul's second request beginning in the middle of verse 17 that builds upon the first.

> That you . . . may have strength to comprehend with all the saints what is the breadth and length and height and depth, and to know the love of Christ that surpasses knowledge.

The core of Paul's second request continues with this idea of love, but now he is not talking about our love rooted in Christ, but Christ's love for us.

He prays once again that we will have strength to be able to do two things. First, in verse 18, Paul requests that we will have strength "to comprehend with all the saints what is the breadth and length and height and depth." The word "comprehend" here literally means "to take hold down upon." It has the idea of deeply comprehending something. Paul is praying that we will really be able to take hold down upon the love of Christ, and oh what a love it is! It is such a love that Paul uses grand terms of measurement to describe it. This love has breadth and length and height and depth. This is a great love that takes real mental anguish to comprehend. I am reminded of the hymn "The Love of God" written by Frederick Lehman. The last stanza of the hymn well reflects this idea of the grandeur of Christ's love.

> Could we with ink the ocean fill,
> And were the skies of parchment made,
> Were every stalk on earth a quill,
> And every man a scribe by trade,
> To write the love of God above,
> Would drain the ocean dry.
> Nor could the scroll contain the whole,
> Though stretched from sky to sky.

Christ's love is immeasurable, and Paul is praying that we would be able to comprehend it.

But intellectual comprehension of Christ's love is not enough. Paul prays also in verse 19 that we would *know* the love of Christ. This is more than mere intellectual knowledge—James tells us that even the demons know that. This is personal, experiential, devotional love. And you can see how this request goes hand in hand with Paul's first request. As our inner man is strengthened and Christ settles down in us, and we are really rooted and grounded in our love for him, we begin to better comprehend and know his love for us. And when we know his love for us better, we are rooted even deeper in our love for him.

This work of the Spirit by which we grow in our love for Christ and in our knowledge of him expands and fills us until the point when we are all-consumed by love for Christ and knowledge of his love! As we grow to know his love, we will grow to love him ultimately with an exclusive, consuming love. Nothing else will compare. All of our other loves and delights will only be to serve our love for Christ. And then we will be able to say with Paul in Philippians 3, "I consider everything a loss compared to the surpassing greatness of knowing Christ Jesus my Lord, for whose sake I have lost all things. I consider them rubbish, that I may gain Christ. . . . I want to know Christ and the power of his resurrection and the fellowship of sharing in his sufferings, becoming like him in his death."

Filled to the Fullness

And as these two requests are answered in our lives and we are more firmly rooted in our love for Christ and we know his love even more, then Paul's third request in verse 19 will be a reality in our lives—we will be filled with all the fullness of God. In other words, our love and delight for God in the person of Jesus Christ will fill us to the brim so that nothing else can occupy the center of our affections! To be filled with God is to have him occupy our affections, and to be filled to measure is to be filled to the degree that nothing else fits.

You see, every true believer does have affection for God, at least to some degree. You cannot be a Christian and not love God. But most, if not all of us, share space in our love for other things as well, and anything we allow to share space in our love with God is an idol for us. Idols compete for our affection. Idols are jealous; they do not like to share space with God. But our God is also jealous! He will not share space in our affections with idols.

If we were to be really honest, we would all have to admit that we have other things competing with our love for Christ. We are not filled to the fullness with God. He occupies our love, but so do other things. And it is this very condition that prevents us from sweet communion with God. This is the essence of your sanctification—having your inner man strengthened by the Spirit so that Christ can progressively settle down in your heart more and more, and you will be more and more rooted and grounded in your love for him. It is growing in your comprehension and personal knowledge of his love. It is being more and more filled with God to the point that all lesser loves are pushed out.

This is what it means to be commune with God. Not mere intellectual beliefs, although those are necessary. Not just working hard to do good things and be right, although that will come. The Christian life is about love for God—it is pursuing communion with Christ.

6

The Fruit of Communion with God

THERE WAS COMMOTION AT the windows. *What are they doing here?* he thought.

He had not expected to meet this famed teacher, let alone dine with him at his table. He had been minding his own business, collecting taxes for the Romans. It was his job; sure, he took a little off the top, but who wouldn't?

But then he had looked up at the next person in line at his tax booth, and there he was—the man everyone was talking about.

"Follow me," he had said, and began walking away.

The man hadn't thought twice; something within his soul compelled him to follow the teacher. So he rose and followed him. He looked behind him as he heard scuffling on the path; others were following, too, and they weren't the greatest kind of people—there was a colleague from the tax guild; that man was an infamous pickpocket; and that woman, she was the type men only saw in private.

After a few moments, he had realized where they were going—*his house!*

"Yes, Lord." He rushed to the teacher's side. "Please, come in and eat at my table."

The teacher had turned to the rest. "Come, all of you, eat with me."

And now, in the middle of this amazing, unexpected meal, religious leaders were crowding the windows, peering in with their pious, self-righteous scowls.

He overheard one of them speak to another of the teacher's followers. "Why does he eat with tax collectors and sinners?"

> Those who are well have no need of a physician,
> but those who are sick.
> I came not to call the righteous, but sinners. (Mark 2:17)

APPROVING GOOD

As we have seen, communion with God in which we faithfully dialogue with God by hearing him in his word and speaking back to him results in hearts filled with affection for God. This in itself is a wonderful result of a life given as a living sacrifice to God.

But remember that Christ also promised that if we abide in him—if we allow his words to abide in us and our words in him—then we will bear much fruit. So what are some of the fruits we will experience as we grow in our devotion to God?

We have already noted that a life given to God as a living sacrifice consists of not being conformed to this world and being transformed by the renewing of our minds, and this renewal takes place exactly because we have immersed our hearts and minds in the Word of God. It is only through the Scriptures that the Spirit of God transforms us.

But notice the primary focus and intent of Romans 12:1–2: we find a purpose clause at the end of verse 2 that indicates to us the reason for the commands in this passage: "that by testing you may discern what is the will of God, what is good and acceptable and perfect." The primary commands in this passage are each leading us toward one goal, that of discerning God's will, that which is good and acceptable and perfect. When we do offer ourselves completely to God as a sacrifice by rejecting the world's values and renewing our minds in the Scriptures, then we will be able to test and discern what is truly good.

This two-step process of testing and discerning is important to understand. They translate one Greek word that carries two important implications. One is the idea of testing something to see if it has value, and the other is being able to recognize and approve of a value when you see it. It's one thing to test something to see if it is valuable, but it's an entirely different thing to be able to recognize its value. It's one thing to be told, "This has value," but it's an entirely different thing to really recognize the value for yourself.

A mark of someone who is growing in his communion with God is being able to test something and then recognize its true spiritual value. It's like the banker who is able to recognize the difference between a counterfeit $100 bill and a real one just by feeling them because he has spent so much time handling the real thing. That's the kind of people we will become as we grow to truly know God through communing with him.

NEW PRIORITIES

Second, making communion with God our first priority results in fruit in other important priorities as well. There are many things in our individual lives and in the lives of our churches that vie for our attention. In our lives we concern ourselves with our families, with our jobs, with paying the bills, and maintaining our homes, and our hobbies, and entertainment—all of these are good, and they have their proper place. In the life of our church we have many different concerns as well: maintaining a building, scheduling our meetings, paying our bills, deciding who is going to bring snacks for fellowship time.

There are many good things in our lives and in our church ministries, but it is important to recognize that the Bible clearly identifies a central concern that is to be always at the top of our list of priorities. And, in fact, as we shall see, it is only when we have made this our top priority that we will be most fruitful in other important areas of our lives and ministries as well.

In John 15, Jesus discussed priorities that should be central in the lives and ministries of his followers. He gives attention to our relationship with the people of God: "Love one another as I have loved you," he commanded (v. 12). He also addresses our relationship with the unbelieving world: He warned his disciples that the world would hate them (v. 18) but that they would be witnesses of him to those who hate them (v. 27). However, the first matter with which Jesus both admonished and encouraged his disciples is what he considers our first priority, what we have already seen explained in verses 1–11: "Abide in me"—communion with God.

It is only *after* Jesus spends time emphasizing the importance and significance of our relationship with him that he then moves in verses 12–17 to talk about a second kind of relationship: our relationship with one another—our second priority:

> This is my commandment, that you love one another as
> I have loved you.

And then in verses 18–27 he transitions to another kind of relationship that should be our concern: our relationship to the world—our third priority:

> And you also will bear witness, because you have been
> with me from the beginning.

The order in which he discusses these relationships is not arbitrary, and in fact, if we get these priorities out of order, we are bound to fail in any of them. In other words, if we make as our primary priority, for example, our relationships with one another as the people of God—if we give first priority to even important things like fellowship or discipleship or the strengthening of our families—we will ultimately fail, because it is only when we nurture and cultivate our relationship with God in Christ *first* that we will be able to rightly build our relationships with other believers. It is only when we allow Christ's words to abide in us and allow our words to abide in him *first* that we will be the kind of people who can rightly relate to other Christians. It is only when we abide in his love, keeping his commandments, that we will successfully bear fruit in our relationships with the people of God.

Or, if we give first priority to our relationships with the world—if we make as our primary priority important matters such as evangelism or missions—we will ultimately fail, because it is only when we make our relationship with God in Christ *first* that we will be the kind of people who can rightly testify, out of our personal experience with God, to those who do not believe.

To put it very simply, it is our first priority—our relationship with God—that motivates us and equips us to bear fruit in our second priority—our relationships with the people of God—and our third priority—our relationships with the world.

FERVENT MISSION

The connection between these three priorities is so because all three are relationships, and it is only when we cultivate our relationship with God that we can nurture a relationship with other Christians and an evangelistic relationship with the unbelieving world. Later in John 17, Jesus explains this connection. Look at verse 20:

> I do not ask for these only, but also for those who will believe in me through their word.

First, we find that just as Christ was commissioned to make God known, so we are commissioned to make Christ known to others. The only way others will believe in Christ is if they are told by us, and that is what we have been commissioned to do. Faith in Jesus comes only through hearing about him.

And, just like Jesus made the Father known through the proclamation of his Word, so we make Christ known through the proclamation of his Word. Faith comes by hearing, and hearing by the Word of God. No one will know Christ, no one will believe in Christ, unless someone proclaims him to them.

We must go into all the world and preach the good news of Jesus Christ, the message that the Son of God became man and lived a perfect life, obeying the law that we could not obey; the message that this perfect God/man sacrificed himself in our place and took the punishment of death that we rightly deserve; the message that this Savior rose from the dead and proved that he had satisfied the wrath of God and offers forgiveness of sin to all who repent of their sin and believe in him. This is the Word that we are commissioned to proclaim to the world.

And notice in verse 21 what happens when people believe our word about Jesus:

> That they may all be one, just as you, Father, are in me, and I in you, that they also may be in us, so that the world may believe that you have sent me.

This belief in Jesus through our word *unifies* these new believers with us into Christ's spiritual body. And what's more, this very unity draws more people in the world to belief! Communion with God and communion with our fellow believers is one of the most potent ways that we make Christ known to the world. And when we add to that display of unity the preached word about Christ's life and death and resurrection, people will believe. According to Christ's words, unity is both produced by the gospel and it is that which will draw others to believe when it is combined with proclamation of the gospel.

Now, we need to stop for a moment and explore what this unity really means, because there is a lot of talk about unity today with little clarification as to what that means biblically. Thankfully, Christ's own statements in this passage clarify what this unity will look like. First, look at verse 14:

> I have given them your Word—that's the Word that we're meant to proclaim as a means to making Christ known to the world—and the world has hated them because they are not of the world, just as I am not of the world.

So whatever this unity is—this unity that will make Christ known to the world—it is a unity that separates us from the world. Now that seems a bit strange. It would seem that if we want to reach the world, we should try to be as much like them as we can be. We should conform ourselves and our message as close as we can to the world so that they can relate to us and we can reach them.

But that's not how Christ presents our mission, and remember, our mission is to do what he tells us to do. He says that our message—his Word—will actually cause the world to hate us; our unity with him and his Word and each other will set us apart from the world. According to him in verses 15–16, we are sent into the world—he doesn't want to remove us from the world because he wants us to make him known to the world, but even though we are sent into the world, we are not *of* the world because he is not *of* the world. In other words, we do not share the world's values, we do not share the world's loves, we do not conform to the world even in our noble desire to reach the world.

Instead, we are sanctified—that means set apart—we are set apart from the world by the truth of his Word. Look at verse 17:

> Sanctify them in the truth; your Word is truth. As you sent me in the world, so I have sent them into the world. And for their sake I consecrate myself, that they also may be sanctified in truth.

So our unity is not a watering down of the truth or a conformity to the behaviors of this world or a minimizing of doctrine so that we can all get along and can reach the world. On the contrary, our unity is with God and with Christ and with one another, and it is based on being distinct from the world and set apart by the truth of the Word.

In other words, this unity that will reveal Christ and draw people to belief in Christ has a boundary, and it has a center. The boundary of this unity is truth—God's truth as expressed in his Word. There is no unity if there is not unity set apart from the world by truth. And the center of this unity is expressed in verses 21–23:

> That they may all be one, just as you, Father, are in me, and I in you, that they also may be in us, so that the world may believe that you have sent me. The glory that you have given me I have given to them, that they may be one even as we are one, I in them and you in me, that they may become perfectly one, so that the world may know that you sent me and loved them even as you love me.

The boundary of this unity is truth, but the center of this unity is profoundly relational. It is so relational that it is illustrated by the relationship between the Father and the Son. This center of unity is a communion with the glory of God; it is being in God and he in us;

it is as he says later, the love of the Father with which he loved the Son being in us, and Christ in us.

To put it very simply, *the center of our unity is communion with God.*

This is what we celebrate in the Lord's Table. The Lord's Table is not *only* a remembrance and proclamation of Christ's death, it is also a visible representation of the *communion* we share with him and with each other as his body. He is the one who invites us to the Table, and he would not do that if there were anything between us and him; and we gather around that Table together, which we would not do if we were not in union.

In 1 Corinthians 11, Paul gives specific instruction to the church concerning participating in the Lord's Supper. But earlier in chapter 10, he explains how this ordinance beautifully portrays our communion with Christ *and* with believers in the church:

> The cup of blessing that we bless, is it not a participation in the blood of Christ? The bread that we break, is it not a participation in the body of Christ? Because there is one bread, we who are many are one body, for we all partake of the one bread.

The word translated "participation" is *koinonia*, the exact same word translated "communion" throughout Scripture. It emphasizes what we have in common as a local church. It emphasizes the unity we have in Christ, and this is why we sometimes refer to the Lord's Supper as "Communion." Participation in the Lord's Table *is* participation with the sacrifice of Christ, and as we share together and partake of the one bread and the one cup, we demonstrate together the unity and fellowship of the body.

This is why the ordinance was given to the church and not just individuals. You don't just have a few friends over and have Communion—this is for the whole body to partake of together. Members of the body of Christ, who have professed that membership through the sign of baptism, and who are living in unity with others in that body, proclaim their unity with Christ and with each other as they share a meal at his Table.

One of the wonderful things about this ordinance is that it connects all three priorities. We come to the Table at the invitation of Jesus Christ in order to be nourished by communion with him. We are not nourished in some mystical way or by eating the actual flesh and drinking the actual blood of Christ. Rather, we are nourished by the words of Christ dwelling in us and through our prayer of thanksgiving for the sacrificial atonement of Christ on our behalf. Ultimately this Table is about our union and fellowship with Jesus Christ.

But we do not come alone. As we draw near to the Table, we come with the people of God, others who have also been invited by Christ to fellowship with him and be nourished by him. This Table is not only about our union and fellowship with Christ; it is also about our union and fellowship with one another as the people of God. That's why Paul warns about coming to this Table when you have broken fellowship with a brother or sister in Christ—to do so is to eat unworthily

And while we do not invite unbelievers to eat at the Table with us, we do welcome them to observe—this is true of our unconverted children at very least, if not others. And thus the Table also serves as a witness to the world. In the Table the world can come to know why God sent Jesus and the fact that God loves us just as he loves his Son. Paul told us that as often as we eat the bread and drink the cup, we proclaim the Lord's death until he comes.

Here, in this one ritual practice, all three priorities are united and beautifully portrayed. And what the Table pictures in microcosm is true for the whole of our lives and churches: when we make our center the worship of God through Christ, two things happen: first, as we draw near to fellowship with God, we become one with one another. And second, that very communion we have with God and with one another causes the world to believe in Christ.

In other words, when we make worship our first priority, that accomplishes our second priority—nurturing our unity one with another—and our third priority—bringing others who are in the world into union with God and with us. Or, we could say it the other way around: our purpose is to make Christ known to the world through the proclamation of his Word so that people would believe in him and be drawn into communion with God and with his people.

This is what we have been commissioned by Christ to do. Just as Christ had to obey his Father's will for him, so Christ in John 17 calls us, his followers, to accomplish the mission he has given to us. And that mission is to make him known to the world. We do that through the proclamation of his Word and through a display of a unity that is set apart from the world by the truth of his Word. And we do this not for its own sake but so that we can draw more and more people into the fellowship and worship and glory of God and in union with us in the church in order to bring him all honor and glory.

7

The Threat to Communion with God

HE SPEWED THE WATER from his mouth. *Disgusting!*

He had recently come from his home in Colossae. There he regularly enjoyed cool, refreshing water from the spring. He had often taken it for granted.

I should have remembered, he thought picking up the cup he had dropped to the ground. *I'm not home anymore.*

The man was on his way from his home town to his brother's house in Hierapolis. As it was a good day's walk, he had decided to stop in Laodicea for a brief rest, a meal, and what he had hoped to be a refreshing drink. Laodicea had an aqueduct that brought water from a cool spring, he had heard. He had expected the same sweet water he enjoyed back home.

"So sorry, sir," the merchant muttered. "The aqueduct has been recently clogged. Leaking everywhere." He took back the cup. "It takes so long for the water to get here, it's often lukewarm."

Oh well, the man thought as he picked up his things to commence his journey. *I'll have to wait until I get to Hierapolis.* He started down the road. *There, at least, I'll enjoy a soothing bath in the water from the hot spring there.*

Would that you were either cold or hot!
So, because you are lukewarm,
and neither hot nor cold,
I will spit you out of my mouth. (Rev 3:15–16)

LUKEWARM CHRISTIANITY

God invites us to draw near to communion with him through faith in the atoning sacrifice of his Son, Jesus Christ. What a wondrous privilege and joy.

But to return to the picture from Revelation 3:20 with which I opened the book, why is Jesus often out on the porch knocking on the front door rather than sitting at our dining table communion with us?

Remember, Christ knocking at the door in Revelation 3 is not an invitation for salvation given to unbelievers, it is an invitation for communion given to Christians. The message in Revelation 3 specifically describes the condition of Christianity in the church at Laodicea that has hindered their communion with God:

> I know your works: you are neither cold nor hot. Would that you were either cold or hot! So, because you are lukewarm, and neither hot nor cold, I will spit you out of my mouth. (Rev 3:15–16)

Now, when he says that he wishes they would be either hot or cold, this does not mean that he wishes they would either be on fire for him or unsaved; God does not desire that any would perish, but that all would come to repentance. This description does not describe spiritual temperature per se, and understanding the context of this city he is addressing will help us understand that.

The city of Laodicea had no fresh water of its own. In order to get fresh water for the city, archeologists have discovered that the Laodiceans built an advanced system of aqueducts that piped water from a distant spring. The problem is that mineral deposits built up in the aqueducts, causing the pipes to get clogged and eventually leak so that by the time the water actually got to the city, it was

putrid and lukewarm. Seven miles north of Laodicea, the city of
Hierapolis had famous hot springs. Ten miles west of Laodicea, the
city of Colossae had fresh cold springs. Hot water was desirable—it
was useful for bathing and cleaning, and the heat burned off im-
purities. Fresh cold water was desirable for drinking. But putrid,
lukewarm, impure water was useless and vomit-inducing.

And this is exactly how Jesus describes the church in Laodicea. They aren't the hot, relaxing, disinfecting waters of Hierapolis,
but neither are they the cool, refreshing springs of Colossae. They
are lukewarm.

Now remember, as is clear from the context, Jesus is describing the condition of their relationship with him. These people were
apparently ambivalent about their relationship with him. They had
prayed the sinners' prayer; they went regularly to church; they didn't
worship idols or spend time in the brothels. They were just fine.
They had all the Jesus they needed to secure their place in heaven;
they didn't need any more.

And what is Christ's response to that kind of Christianity?
He is going to vomit them out of his mouth. Imagine picking up a
glass of water on hot day, expecting a refreshing drink, putting the
glass to your lips, and tasting putrid lukewarm water. You would
spew that out of your mouth, and that is exactly what Jesus thinks
of these people.

Now this is where it gets a bit disconcerting. This doesn't
sound like true Christianity. Jesus's reaction doesn't sound like how
he would react to a true child of his. There is some debate about
whether these people in Laodicea were truly Christians or not; I'll
leave that for you to decide. But either way, this is not how you want
Jesus to describe your relationship with him.

Yet the problem with this church is not just their spiritual
condition; it's the fact that they don't even recognize their problem.
Look at how he further describes them in verse 17:

> For you say, I am rich, I have prospered, and I need noth-
> ing, not realizing that you are wretched, pitiable, poor,
> blind, and naked.

Laodicea was a very wealthy city. It was at a commercial crossroads; it was a banking center; it was famous for its shiny, black wool; it had a well-known medical school that produced a special ointment that cured eye defects. These people needed nothing.

And that's exactly what they thought regarding their relationship with Christ as well. "We have everything we need. We're on our way to heaven. We've got our ticket." They're self-righteous, self-satisfied; they need nothing.

And they couldn't have been more wrong. They think they're rich spiritually, Jesus says they are wretched, pitiable, poor; they think they're spiritually healthy, Jesus says they are blind; they think they are clothed in warm wool, Jesus says they're naked; again, it's hard to see how he could be describing true Christians here.

INORDINATE AFFECTIONS

Paul warned Timothy about exactly this problem, characterizing a time in which a significant threat against communion with God will arise: "But understand this, that in the last days there will come times of difficulty" (2 Tim 3:1). Now what is interesting about this warning is that he has just cautioned Timothy about false teachers who would attack doctrine, only to follow with, *But understand this.* There is something that is an even greater danger to Christianity than false teachers opposing the truth. There is something that is going to be true of the last days that will be even more terrible.

We are in these last days. Hebrews 1 says that "long ago, at many times and in many ways, God spoke to our fathers by the prophets, but *in these last days* he has spoken to us by his Son." Christ's coming to earth marked the beginning of the last days. Peter made this clear in Acts 2 when he said that Joel's prophesy about the last days began to be fulfilled when the Holy Spirit came on the day of Pentecost. So we are in the last days. The great danger that Paul describes here applies to us, and in fact, the word Paul uses in verse 1 for "times" could be translated "era," indicating that each additional era will grow more and more terrible.

So what is it in these last days that is such a danger to the church? Paul describes this danger with a list of eighteen vices beginning in verse 2 and continuing through verse 4. He adds an additional quality of these terrible times with a participle phrase in verse 5 that modifies the entire list of vices—"having the appearance of godliness, but denying its power."

So what is so terrible about these last days? We may think that Paul is being a bit overdramatic until we recognize that Paul is not talking about the world, he is talking about professing Christians. This list describes not the sinful people of this world, but professing believers inside the church, those who have "the appearance of godliness."

In other words, the greatest threat to true communion with God is a kind of false, external appearance of communion with God. And according to Paul's description here, what constitutes false communion is with God is inordinate affections—a kind of "lukewarm" love for him.

Consider how Paul describes this danger to genuine Christianity beginning in verse 2 of 2 Timothy 3. The first two characteristics are clearly connected: "lovers of self" and "lovers of money." In the Greek the connection is even more vivid, each word beginning with a form of *phileo*, which means to have great affection. Here you can see already clear examples of inordinate affections. The last description Paul gives in verse 4 is "lovers of pleasure rather than lovers of God." Again, the Greek clearly demonstrates the connection with the first two vices. So already you can see that these bookend characteristics set the tone for the whole list. The entire list is about inordinate affection—loving the wrong things, loving good things too much, or loving the right things in the wrong way.

Now, it may not seem obvious why inordinate affection is a problem until we remember that affections are at the heart of communion with God; failure to respond toward God with right affection is a failure to worship him as he deserves, and consequently, a failure to bring him glory. So inordinate affection in the form of loving the wrong things is idol worship. Inordinate affection in the form of loving good things too much is idol worship. And even inordinate affection in the form of loving the right things in the wrong way is idol worship. So obviously, any kind of love that leads to idol worship is a great danger!

Most of the characteristics of false communion that Paul lists are fairly obvious, but they help to demonstrate how these inordinate affections take form. For instance, consider the first one— "lovers of self." There is a sense in which all people love themselves. For instance, Paul tells men in Ephesians to love their wives just like they love themselves (Eph 5:28). But your affection for yourself becomes inordinate when you begin to love yourself so much that you do things for yourself and you ignore others and God.

Or how about "love of money"? God has given us material possessions to enjoy and use as tools, but when we love money so much because of what it can do for us, our love becomes inordinate. This is why Paul warned Timothy in his first letter that the love of money is the root of all kinds of evil (1 Tim 6).

The next three terms describe pride and hostility toward others. Being "proud," "arrogant," and "abusive" toward others exhibits a misguided love. The Bible commands us to love our neighbors as ourselves. When we fail in this, we reveal inordinate affection.

All but one of the next nine vices make use of a prefix similar to our English prefixes "un" or "dis," which reverse an action. For instance, if someone is *not* kind, he is "*un*kind." Or if you do *not* like something, then you "*dis*like" it. This Greek prefix is reflected in English with most of the terms in the text, and Paul used this grammatical construction to further illustrate inordinate affection—in this case, taking something that is good and doing the opposite.

For instance, look at the next one—"*dis*obedient to parents." Obedience demonstrates proper love and respect for parents. Doing the opposite reveals inordinate affection for our parents. What about "*un*grateful"? We have already seen how critically important the affection of gratitude is to genuine communion with God. *In*gratitude is inordinate affection. "*Un*holy" carries the sense of being grossly indecent or having impropriety. Again, misguided affection leaves us with little discernment or propriety concerning how we should act or what we should love. The next vice, "heart*less*," has specific reference to family love. So here the vice is loving something good— family—the wrong way. Inordinate affection. "*Un*appeasable" reveals inordinate affection in that we do not love the other person and we do not love peace and reconciliation enough to forgive. We love ourselves too much. We have to make a point or we demand our rights instead of being willing to forgive unconditionally for the sake of the other person. This is inordinate affection!

Already we should begin taking stock of ourselves. Do you see any of these vices within yourself? Do you see within yourself self-love, love of money, pride, abusiveness, ungratefulness, or lack of love toward your family?

And then, smack in the middle of this list, is a word unlike any of the others. Paul has been listing all of these "uns"—"ungrateful, unholy, unloving, unforgiving," and then he uses the term *diaboloi*. The ESV says "slanderous," but to better reflect the original Greek, we could say, "diabolical." Now what is interesting about this term is that it is a form of the word for "devil," the same word that was used at the end of chapter 2 to describe the devil's hold on those who accept doctrinal heresy.

It's almost as if at the middle of this list of vices in the church, Paul is telling us that the same root cause of doctrinal heresy—the devil—is the root cause of inordinate affection. This is serious! Here are professing believers—those who claim to be in communion with God—who have inordinate affections, and the root cause is "devilishness!" These vices describe *Christians*? Do these vices describe *you*?

It seems as if the next six vices get worse and worse, spiraling into unbelievable devilishness. "*Un*controlled," "*un*tamed," "*un*loving of good," "treacherous," "reckless, "and "swollen with conceit." These are not vices of the world, these are vices within the church! No wonder Paul says that these last days will be "terrible times"!

And then Paul bookends his list of vices of inordinate affection in verse 4 with "lovers of pleasure rather than lovers of God." This is the ultimate expression of inordinate affection. God, who is all-worthy of our greatest love, is rejected for fleeing earthy pleasure!

This is the most crucial point: We *cannot* love God like we should—we cannot commune with him—when our minds and hearts are so crowded by *lesser* loves. When we love the wrong things, or when we love a good thing too much, or when we love the right things in the wrong way, we *cannot* love God rightly. This is why inordinate affection is such a serious danger against the church, perhaps even more dangerous than attacks against doctrine.

To put it another way, when we fill our dining room full of lesser loves, there is no longer any room for Jesus at our communion table.

If we do not guard ourselves against the enemy of inordinate affections, we will begin to witness the kinds of vices Paul has listed in this text. We must guard ourselves against those things that debase our affections. We must guard ourselves against loving lesser things.

If we do not—if we do not fight against inordinate affections—then we will fall prey to what Paul describes in verse 5: "having the appearance of godliness, but denying its power."

EMPTY CHRISTIANITY

At first glance, this charge may not seem to be very serious. But consider what Paul is saying about many professing believers in churches during the last days. Paul says that such people have only the *form* of godliness. They only *look* like they are in communion with God on the outside, but in reality they are not.

There are some people who know what the form of a Christian looks like, and they know very well how to make themselves look a Christian. But they are just wearing a mask, a costume, they are just pretending. They know all the right things to do and all the right things to say to look like a Christian, but it is only a farce.

Is this as serious a charge as it sounds? Yes it is. If you say you love God, but you love lesser things more, or you love God in the wrong way, or you love the wrong things, then you do not love God. Christ himself said in Matthew 6:24, "No one can serve two masters, for either he will hate the one and love the other, or he will be devoted to the one and despise the other. You cannot serve God and money." Love for God and inordinate affection are mutually exclusive. You cannot have both. Either you love God rightly, or you do not. It's that serious.

Paul says that in the last days—in *these* last days—there will be professing Christians who have inordinate affections. They love the wrong things, they love good things too much, and they love good things in the wrong way. And these inordinate affections reveal themselves in all kinds of un-Christian vices. These people do not have real godliness, no true communion with God. They are wearing only a mask.

Paul continues in verse 5 by saying that although they have a form of godliness, these professing believers deny its power. This word *deny* is a strong word. It is the same word used in 1 Timothy 5:8 concerning those who "deny the faith," not verbally or not by denying some essential Christian doctrine, but they deny the faith with their actions. The same is true in this passage. By loving wrongly, these people do not really love God. Instead, they have only a form of godliness, and in effect, they deny the power of godliness.

How is it that they deny godliness? Well, true communion with God—true godliness that comes from miraculous regeneration—always results in progressive sanctification. True believers love God. Oh, they may love him imperfectly, but they do love him, and their love for him will increase day by day as they rid themselves of lesser loves. True believers reject loving those things that are unworthy of love. True believers fight against the kinds of vices listed in this text. True believers exhibit ordinate affection for God!

So when someone says that he is a Christian—that he is in communion with God, and he yet exhibits inordinate affection through vices like those in this text; when people like this play the part of a Christian on the outside but yet insist on loving the wrong things and loving the right things wrongly; when they *say* that they are pursuing communion with God but do not live like it; then they in a sense deny that godliness has any power to change lives. They deny that a changed life will result in changes action. They deny that a changed heart will result in changed loves. They deny the power of godliness.

And you can only leave Jesus out on the porch for so long.

8

The Recovery of
Communion with God

WHAT IS HE DOING?

The servant stared with bewilderment as his master girded up his garment and bent down to the bowl of water. He had done as his lord had commanded—he was dressed and ready for service; the lamps were burning, even though it was already the third watch. He was still awake.

He had sprung to his feet the moment he heard the knock at the door. He had opened the door to find his master standing, weary from the long feast and the hard journey home, but with a look of approval on his face.

"Well done, my servant," the master had said, handing his cloak and saddle bag to the servant.

"Welcome home, lord," the servant had exclaimed, moving quickly back as his master entered the house. He shut the door and laid the things aside. "Everything is ready. You must be exhausted." He moved toward the inner chambers. "Come, I will help you prepare to retire."

But his master had not followed him; instead, he had turned aside toward the dining room.

What is he doing?

Following behind his master, the servant watched as he dressed himself for service. He carefully washed his hands in the basin, drying them on the cloth lying beside it. He turned to the servant.

"Come, my faithful servant," he said, gesturing to the table. "Recline at table, and I will come and serve you."

> Blessed are those servants whom the master finds
> awake when he comes.
> Truly, I say to you, he will dress himself for service
> and have them recline at table,
> and he will come and serve them. (Luke 12:37)

OPEN THE DOOR

Laodicea was a real city in Asia Minor, and the church in Revelation 3 was a real church, and Jesus sent the letter through John to this real church in this real city. But there's also something about the description of this church that rings true today, too, doesn't it?

Here is a church of professing Christians who are wealthy and comfortable and safe and self-righteous and complacent and lukewarm and indifferent about their fellowship with Jesus Christ. Here is a people who needed Christ for their salvation, but now they think they need nothing.

Does that sound at all like twenty-first century Christianity? Does that sound at all like us at times? It certainly describes me more often than I'd like to admit.

Perhaps you've begun to recognize inordinate affection in your life; maybe you've identified some idols that are crowding out your love for Christ and joy in him; perhaps you find yourself lacking the God-glorifying gratitude he deserves. You look at your table of communion, and Christ is not sitting there. Perhaps you're worried and scared—*Am I a Christian at all?*

If that's you, then praise the Lord. If you're worried, then that's already an act of grace. If you're concerned that your joy is not in Christ, then God is already doing a work in your heart. If you don't care—if you have no joy in Christ and that does not bother you, then you should be concerned.

But perhaps you do realize that you do not commune with Christ like you should. What should you do?

CHRIST'S SOLUTION

Jesus's condemnation upon his church in Revelation 3—a situation Paul predicted would come in these last days—is very sober, very troubling. They are sickening to him, and they don't even realize it.

And yet, Jesus does not leave it there, and this may give us cause to believe that those to whom he wrote in Laodicea really were truly Christians after all. He doesn't judge them, condemn them, and leave them where they are. Rather, he gives them a very direct, very stern warning, but then he offers a solution and pleads with them to restore the broken communion that their indifference has caused.

> I counsel you to buy from me gold refined by fire, so that you may be rich, and white garments so that you may clothe yourself and the shame of your nakedness may not be seen, and salve to anoint your eyes, so that you may see. Those whom I love, I reprove and discipline, so be zealous and repent. Behold, I stand at the door and knock. If anyone hears my voice and opens the door, I will come in to him and eat with him, and he with me. (Rev 3:18–20)

Christ's counsel to the Laodiceans—and to us—is so important, and truly loving. Because if you are poor, what do you need to solve your problem? Well, you need money, so just go out and work. But what if you're also blind? You can't see to work, so how do you solve your problem? Well, maybe you can just go out and beg; surely you can get some money that way.

But what if you're also naked? I mean, you can't even leave your house. What can you do then? The answer is, you can't do anything for yourself. You have no solution. You have no hope.

So Jesus provides the solution himself.

Isn't this an amazing reality? Here are people, people for whom Christ died, people who have taken advantage of his atonement for their sins, people who claim his name but are indifferent toward him; they think they are rich and clothed and healthy when they are really poor and blind and naked. They are sickening to Christ; he wants to spew them out of his mouth. And Jesus says, "Come back to me. I want to help you. In fact, I am going to provide the solution for you."

That is grace.

He says in verse 18: "You think you're rich already, but I counsel you to buy from *me* gold refined by fire, so that you may be rich—you need *my* gold." You don't need material wealth; you need the riches of Christ! You think you're already clothed, but you don't need that shiny black wool, you need the "white garments of Christ so that you may clothe yourself and the shame of your nakedness may not be seen." These are robes that have been made white by the blood of the Lamb.

"You think you've got all the medicine you need in your fancy medical schools, but you need *my* salve to anoint your eyes, so that you may see." Don't rely on yourselves; don't be self-satisfied; you need something better. The solution for those who are poor and blind and naked and indifferent and lukewarm is to stretch out their hand and take hold of what Christ has already provided—his riches, his righteousness, his healing power.

This is not a harsh condemnation of a pitiless judge! This is a hope-filled plea from a scorned father who loves his children deeply and desperately desires for restored fellowship and communion with them. His relationship with his children has been broken due to their self-righteousness and indifference, but he longs once again to have that sweet communion they once shared.

And so he does what it takes. He does what any loving father would do—he reproves them; he disciplines them; he pleads with them to repent and turn back to him. We who are parents know exactly what this is like, don't we? There have been times when one of my children has disobeyed and is having a bad attitude and I've looked them in the face and said, "I am on your side. Stop resisting me. I want to help you!" They think we're punishing them because we hate them, but nothing could be further from the truth. We love them so deeply and just want our relationship restored!

And that's what Jesus wants.

He is an estranged father, locked out of his son's house. His son is in there, he thinks he's wealthy and healthy and clothed when in reality he is poor and blind and naked.

And Jesus knocks on the door, and he says, "I want to come in to you. I want to dine with you. Look, I'll bring the meal, I'll bring the gold, I'll bring the pure white garments, I'll bring the salve for your blind eyes. I want to commune with you once again."

And all that is required is that we repent of our indifference and our lukewarmness and embrace his riches, relying once again on his righteous garments, opening our eyes once again to the beauties of his mercy and grace. Welcome him to your table; listen to him talk in his Word; speak to him in prayer.

A LIFE OF COMMUNION

So how does this affect us practically in our personal lives and in the lives of our churches? Here are a few suggestions.

We begin first with our personal lives. We must make abiding in Christ our first and ultimate priority, and we have already seen what this will look like. We will fill ourselves with his words. We will spend time reading and meditating upon the Word of God, allowing its truths to fill us. We will fill Christ with our words. We will spend time in prayer, making our requests known to him, sharing part of ourselves with him, and casting all our burdens upon him. And we will abide in his love by keeping his commandments. We will recognize that obedience to his commands is not optional or secondary; rather it is how we abide in the love of Jesus and how we prove that we are his disciples.

Why, Oh, why do we spend our lives pursuing things that have no lasting value? Why are we so concerned with what unbelievers think about us or how popular we are or how accepted we are in the world? Don't you realize that if you give all of that up you can have Christ? Give it up! Forsake the world! Forsake yourself! Forsake the fleeting pleasures of this world.

Run to Christ! Gaze upon Christ! Put your faith in Christ! Love Christ! Delight in Christ!

Beg the Lord to give you deep affection for Christ. Not joy in things, not just love for itself, but love and joy in Christ. Fall on your face before your Savior and repent of delighting in things other than him, and beg him to fill you with an inexpressible and glorious joy in him. As we saw earlier, God is the source of our affection for him. Unless he creates light in our hearts, we will not have this love and joy in him. So ask him for it.

We must make abiding in Christ the first priority of our families as well. Making dinner, cleaning the house, working in the yard, are all good and necessary things, but we must make family worship and nurturing relationship with God primary in our homes. Stimulate your spouse to abide in Christ; guide your children to communion with him through the gospel and regular, family worship. And then we will allow this first priority of abiding in Christ to fuel and equip us for our relationships with others and with the world. Success in those areas is directly dependent upon our relationship with God.

What about our church life? It is important that an understanding of what we have been discussing be the driving force behind any philosophy of ministry. It is so easy for churches to get sidetracked with so many different ministries and priorities—even good and necessary things. But the first priority of any church should be to nurture Christians' relationship with God through Christ, and churches do that primarily through corporate worship. Our worship services are not simply *expressions* of our relationship with God; our services *form* and *shape* our relationship with him. This affects how we worship and the emphasis we place on worship in a church. It's the reason worship services should begin and end with God's Word. It's why the structure of a service should be a dialogue between God and us. It's why church services should contain abundant Scripture—God's words abiding in us—and prayers—our words abiding in God. The structure of our services, the songs we sing, the Scriptures we read, the prayers we pray—everything about our services shapes our minds and our hearts to be the kind of people who are abiding in Christ to the greatest degree.

Historically, church worship services have been designed in such a way to both display and nurture this kind of communion by being structured as a dialogue. God speaks, we respond. God speaks to reveal himself to us and call us to worship, we respond with praise and adoration. God speaks to remind us of our sin and unworthiness, we respond with confession. God speaks words of pardon through Christ, we respond with thanksgiving. God speaks words of instruction to us, we respond with dedication. God speaks a charge and blessing upon us, we respond by going out in obedience. This dialogical nature of corporate communion in worship services is meant to shape us into people who will commune with God like this regularly as individuals in private times of communion, and as families in times of family devotion.

As we have seen, we must remember that it is only when we make worship our first priority that we will be able to bear fruit in our discipleship and fellowship ministries and in evangelism and missions. As important as those ministries are, and they are very important—Christ commanded that they be part of what we do as a church—we will fail at them unless they flow out of our relationship with God through Christ.

Our first priority as Christians and as churches must be an active pursuit of a living and vital relationship with God through Jesus Christ. We must abide in him. His words must abide in us as we lift our prayers to him. We must abide in his love by obeying his commandments. And if we pursue this as individual Christians and in our primary meetings as churches, we will grow in union with one another, accomplishing our second priority, and in our witness to the world, our third priority.

WELCOME HOME

It is unfortunately so easy to become indifferent about our relationship with Christ, isn't it? This is especially true when from all outward appearances, we don't really need him. I mean, we recognize that we need him for our salvation, but we're fairly comfortable, we feel pretty safe, we're healthy; we've got cozy homes and good families and stable jobs. What more do we need?

It's often not until we lose something, or we find ourselves in desperation, that we recognize once again our daily need of communion with God. And that may be exactly what we need sometimes. God may have to discipline us by removing something of comfort to cause us to recognize that we need him. So if you lose something, there may be many reasons God has done that in your life, but at least one question you should ask is whether that loss is the sound of knocking at your door. Whether it is Jesus calling you back to the communion with him that perhaps you have grown indifferent toward.

But it really shouldn't need to take that kind of loss. We need to develop the habit of dining with Christ regularly, whether we "feel" like we need him or not. And we must place an emphasis on our corporate worship, which forms and shapes spiritual disciplines within us that will make us a people who regularly communion with God each and every day.

And this is why the Lord's Table—Communion—is so important and why historically churches have practiced it with far more regularity than most churches do today. The Lord's Table is Christ himself inviting us to *his* table in *his* dining room in *his* house so that we might commune with him through his sacrifice of atonement; it is the most beautiful picture we have of everything we have been talking about in this book.

So if you find that you have grown lukewarm, you have grown indifferent to your relationship with God, what is the solution? The solution is not to condemn and judge or self-pity and beat ourselves up. The answer is simply to repent. The answer is to embrace the riches and beauty of Christ once again. Take advantage of those spiritual disciplines that God has ordained as a means to cultivating our relationship with him—regular Bible study, fervent prayer, faithful participation in corporate worship.

The answer is to simply open the door. Welcome him back into your home. Invite him into your dining room. Sit across the table from him—the Table that he himself prepared with his broken body and shed blood—sit at his Table, and commune with him.

www.ingramcontent.com/pod-product-compliance
Lightning Source LLC
Chambersburg PA
CBHW060424090426
42734CB00011B/2444